THE PERMANENT REVOLUTION
CHANGE I

| THE RITE OF I AND THOU | → | THE VISION OF UNDOING THE MYTH OF EDEN | → | THE STREET: |

THE REVOLUTION OF BEING
GLIMPSES OF THE POST-REVOLUTIONARY WORLD

| THE RITE OF NEW POSSIBILITIES | → | THE VISION OF LANDING ON MARS | → | HANOI/SAIGON: THERE IS A GROUP LIVING IN AN ANARCHIST SOCIETY. WHAT ARE THEY DOING? |

THE REVOLUTION OF TRANSFORMATION
THE STRUGGLE PERIOD

| THE RITE OF OPPOSITE FORCES | → | THE VISION OF THE MAGIC LOVE ZAP | → | CAPETOWN/BIRMINGHAM: THE BLACKS ARE CONFRONTING THE WHITES WITH REVOLUTION. HOW DO THEY OVERCOME? |

THE REVOLUTION OF ACTION
THE PLAN GOES INTO EFFECT. BURN THE MONEY

| THE RITE OF THE MYSTERIOUS VOYAGE | → | THE VISION OF THE INTEGRATION OF THE RACES | → | PARIS: TIME FUTURE: THE NON-VIOLENT ANARCHIST REVOLUTION |

THE SEXUAL REVOLUTION : THE EXORCISM OF VIOLENCE
ATTOKATASTASIS: THE TRANSFORMATION OF DEMONIC FORCES INTO THE CELESTIAL

| THE RITE OF UNIVERSAL INTERCOURSE | → | THE VISION OF APOKATASTASIS | → | JERUSALEM: THE VICTIMS BECOME EXECUTIONERS. WHAT DO THE PACIFISTS DO? |

THE REVOLUTION OF GATHERED FORCES

| THE RITE OF STUDY | → | THE VISION OF THE CREATION OF LIFE | → | JUST KNOW: THERE IS A GROUP OF PEOPLE WHO WANT TO CHANGE THE WORLD |

THE REVOLUTION OF REVELATION
THE DESTINATION MUST BE MADE CLEAR

| THE RITE OF PRAYER | → | THE VISION OF THE DISCOVERY OF THE NORTH POLE | → | BOLIVIA: A GROUP OF REVOLUTIONARIES PLOT THEIR STRATEGY |

THE REVOLUTION OF CULTURES
THE CULTURE MUST BE CHANGED. PERCEPTION MUST BE CHANGED
SO THAT THE USEFULNESS OF THE REVOLUTION CAN BE COMPREHENDED

| THE RITE OF GUERILLA THEATRE | → | THE VISION OF THE DEATH AND RESURRECTION OF THE AMERICAN INDIAN | → | NEW YORK CITY: 8,000,000 PEOPLE ARE LIVING IN A STATE OF EMERGENCY |

The Living Theatre
: *USA*

The Living Theatre
:USA

Renfreu Neff

**The Bobbs-Merrill Company
Indianapolis and New York**

The Bobbs-Merrill Company, Inc.
A Subsidiary of Howard W. Sams & Co., Inc.
Publishers   Indianapolis/Kansas City/New York

© 1970   Renfreu Neff
Library of Congress catalog card number: 71-98292
Manufactured in the United States of America
First printing 1970

Photographs by Gianfranco Mantegna
Body, binding and jacket designed by Aldo Rostagno

for Gianfranco Mantegna

Introduction

From a voyeuristic Pop contact on Pier 40, New York City when the Living Theatre disembarked, I would, one week later, take part in what could easily have been the most beautiful theatrical experience ever to have taken place. This was the opening of *Mysteries and Smaller Pieces* in New Haven. I had never felt such love and excitement in a theatre before, had never seen an audience so completely turned around by a performance as it had been that night. Though some critics and writers had been able to express that sensation in enviably lucid appraisals, their underlying tone was more passionate than usual, and one sensed that, verbally coordinated as they were, they, too, had been moved in some psychic, superconscious area that may never have been touched before.

I empathized with these journalists who had tried to maintain a modicum of editorial decorum in the face of something that had grabbed them on such a spontaneously intimate, mind-blowing level, and if the stark geometric precision of *Antigone* rendered it somewhat less difficult to discuss, *Frankenstein* would register in some fantastic region that defied all literal encapsulation. The problem is that it is easier to explain why one dislikes something than to verbalize one's attraction for something else. One says almost reflexively I don't like that *because* . . . , or it's all right *but* . . . , and possibly because we have been conditioned to want perfection, the put-downs flow effortlessly, as if we have been personally affronted by whatever it was that has failed to reach our presumptive "standards." It is when an experience affects us so deeply, so completely, and moves us beyond where we were in the beginning that verbalization becomes awkward, even meaningless, for the conscious "standards," our crazy expectations, have been shattered; we are caught joyously off-guard, and the only consummate response is yes.

Yes.

Non-verbalization . . . no, call it intuition . . . has never been accepted as a valid basis for convincing a publisher to come across with an advance that will allow a writer to disappear for several months with no assurance that either you or a manuscript will appear at a deadline proposed purely in the interest of filling in at least one blank. Nor is much comfort offered when the subject is a politically oriented theatre group that calls for a revolution that would, among other things, bring about the end of the money system. You explain that the return of the Living Theatre is a "theatrical event," which happens to be true; the editor counters with a noncommittal comment to the effect that it is "perhaps something else," which also happens to be true. And as the euphemisms are cautiously volleyed back and forth, in the back of your mind you dig that since men reject female intuition anyway, a lapse of that faculty would probably be forgivable in the event that the six months really added up to a "theatrical event" and the end result was an amusing display of movable type. You also dig that most books are unforgivable, so in a perverse way you're ahead already, no matter which way the balance falls.

But you also know that you're stalling for time, and as soon as the superlatives have been exhausted, the press release jargon of "incredibles" and "beautifuls" hopefully forgotten and forgiven, it will be possible to formulate a sound reason, based on intuition but not totally dependent upon it.

This reason was to be provided serendipitously through *Paradise Now,* whose deceptively random structure seemed to have entrapped the performers in an unbearably self-indulgent catharsis that exposed the weaknesses of both the company in general and its ideology in particular. *Paradise* was the point at which art and ideology were no longer ingeniously integrated, and in this sense it was the first purely political production of the Living Theatre. In moving out into the audience, possessed of neither the ritual cohesiveness of *Mysteries,* the visual impact of *Frankenstein,* nor the interdependent stability of *Antigone, Paradise* diffused itself in chaos and confusion and became subservient to the audience. For this reason *Paradise* could not be dismissed as readily as one might wish: it functioned as the vehicle that would move the Living Theatre into the revolutionary parallel culture and bring it face to face with a newer and more radicalized phenomenon.

The Living Theatre laid rightful claim to a significant and influential position in the cultural vanguard; moreover, it had sustained that pre-eminence for two generations. This had been a hard-earned experience that should not have been so gratuitously sacrificed by self-righteously turning away from those who questioned or opposed their doctrine—*"If our experience is destroyed, our behaviour will be destructive"*: Laing.[1]

For all of the ideological friction between these two moving forces and their impatience with each other's methods, the goals of both were the same; as the genesis of both was the same, and each in its own way shared and struggled to channel the same turbulent energy that had sprung from the identical geographic chance . . . the Living Theatre and this vociferous young element were uniquely American products. The tour would become a test of one American phenomenon against another.

[1]R. D. Laing, *The Politics of Experience* (London: Penguin Books), 1967.

Part One
In the Beginning

The Living Theatre
Premieres and Openings

At the home of the Becks, 789 West End Ave., New York:

1-4. Four Plays: Paul Goodman's *Childish Jokes,* Gertrude Stein's *Ladies Voices,* Bertoldt Brecht's *He Who Says Yes and He Who Says No,* Federico Garcia Lorca's *The Dialogue of the Manikin and the Young Man* (August 15, 1951).

At the Cherry Lane Theatre, 38 Commerce St., New York:

5. Stein's *Doctor Faustus Lights the Lights* (December 2, 1951).

6. Kenneth Rexroth's *Beyond the Mountains* (December 30, 1951).

7-8. An Evening of Bohemian Theatre: Pablo Picasso's *Desire Trapped by the Tail* (Stein's *Ladies Voices*), T. S. Eliot's *Sweeney Agonistes* (March 2, 1952).

9. Goodman's *Faustina* (May 25, 1952).

10-11. Alfred Jarry's *Ubu the King,* John Ashbery's *The Heroes* (August 5, 1952).

At the attic on 100th St., New York:

12. W. H. Auden's *The Age of Anxiety* (March 18, 1954).

13. Auguste Strindberg's *The Spook Sonata* (June 3, 1954).

14. Jean Cocteau's *Orpheus* (September 30, 1954).

15. Claude Frederick's *The Idiot King* (December 2, 1954).

16. Luigi Pirandello's *Tonight We Improvise* (February 17, 1955).

17. Racine's *Phedre* (May 27, 1955).

3

18.   Goodman's *The Young Disciple* (October 12, 1955).

At the Living Theatre Playhouse, 530 Sixth Ave at 14th St., New York:

19.   William Carlos Williams' *Many Loves* (January 13, 1959).

20.   Goodman's *The Cave at Machpelah* (June 30, 1959).

21.   Jack Gelber's *The Connection* (July 15, 1959).

22.   Pirandello's *Tonight We Improvise* (November 6, 1959).

23-24. The Theatre of Chance: Jackson MacLow's *The Marrying Maiden,* Ezra Pound's *The Women of Trachis* from Sophocles (June 22, 1960).

25.   Brecht's *In the Jungles of Cities* (December 20, 1960).

26.   Gelber's *The Apple* (December 7, 1961).

27.   Brecht's *Man Is Man* (September 18, 1962).

28.   Kenneth H. Brown's *The Brig* (May 15, 1963). Also played for 2 months at Midway Theatre, West 42nd Street, New York, after the federal seizure of the Living Theatre playhouse (October 1963).

Created by the Living Theatre in Europe:

29.   Collective creation *Mysteries and Smaller Pieces* (October 26, 1964, American Center for Students and Artists, Paris).

30.   Jean Genet's *The Maids* (February 26, 1965, Forum Theatre, Berlin).

31.   Collective creation *Frankenstein* from Mary Shelley and film versions (September 26, 1965, commissioned by the Venice Biennale Festival, Teatro La Perla, Lido).

32.   Brecht's *Antigone* from Sophocles (February 19, 1967, Stadttheater, Krefeld, Germany).

4

33. Collective creation *All' Italia* (November 17, 1967, Theatre Français, Bordeaux, the only showing).

34. Collective creation *Paradise Now* (July 24, 1968, Cloitre des Carmes, Avignon, France, commissioned by the Avignon Festival).

In the summer of 1964 the Living Theatre left the United States and began its voluntary exile in Europe. In the creative environment of New York where climate is controlled by money, it was a departure that marked the end of a thirteen-year conflict between artistic integrity and the unrelenting odds against its survival. The Living Theatre's struggle culminated in October of 1963 with government seizure and the closing of its Fourteenth Street theatre premises for failure of its directors, Julian Beck and Judith Malina, to pay federal excise and payroll taxes. Estimated by the Internal Revenue Service at close to $29,000 ($28,435.10), the actual amount, that is, exclusive of penalties and interests attached over a period from 1959 to 1963, was said to be less than $11,000. The Becks had failed to pay these taxes because they could not pay them, not as a protest, and prior to 1959 they had met this responsibility. In the four years that followed there had been numerous exchanges of correspondence between Julian and the IRS, the objective of the former being to show that the Living Theatre was indeed a nonprofit organization, while the latter was apparently concerned with collecting taxes on profits that didn't exist.

7

The group occupied the upper three stories of a small building located on the corner of 14th Street and Sixth Avenue (it has since been razed to make room for a modern structure), but the theatre itself had a seating capacity of only 162; ticket prices were kept low so that everyone could afford to come, and much of the time admission was by donation. There were no "profits," only performance proceeds from which overhead and operating expenses had to be paid before the remainder could be equally divided among the actors. Where taxes were concerned, it came down to a choice between eviction from the theatre and even more extreme personal and artistic deprivation or kicking into the national kitty for armaments and intergalactic hardware. It takes about four seconds of rational rumination to sweat that one out.

And on October 16, 1963 Internal Revenue agents closed the theatre and seized its contents as government property. The actors staged a sit-in inside of the locked premises, friends and patrons picketed on the sidewalk outside, journalists, critics, artists, and intellectuals gave fervent support, and petitions were circulated to keep the Living Theatre alive. Having been refused permission to continue performances of the current production, *The Brig,* and having also discovered an unsealed entrance into the theatre, the actors sneaked into the theatre, erected the set which the agents had dismantled before leaving for the weekend, and gave a "secret" performance before an audience that had managed to enter the building by an unlocked fire exit, through windows and through an opening on the roof.

Though it was said that the Becks had neglected even to

8

file tax returns in the four-year period (the filing of a return unaccompanied by payment considered tantamount to an official IOU in which the taxpayer acknowledges his debt but can't do anything about it), there was nevertheless something over-reactive in the IRS's procedure. From amidst protest and support came speculations that the theatre had been ordered closed because of the anti-Marine content of *The Brig*, and many viewed the government's move as a retaliatory action against the Becks' outspoken pacifistic and anarchistic position, their activism in peace and disarmament movements, and their participation and leadership in numerous nonviolent demonstrations and peace marches—an activism, participation and leadership that had led to their arrests for civil disobedience on countless occasions. All of these speculations were well founded, for neither during nor after the closing of the theatre did the IRS indicate that its primary interest was collecting the money, and at government auction the theatre's physical assets brought only $267 toward the monies owed.

In January and February of 1964, under the corporate name of Exile Productions, the Living Theatre re-opened *The Brig* at the Midway Theatre, but little money was taken in during that two-month run.

In January, the Becks were indicted by a Federal grand jury on eleven counts carrying a maximum penalty of thirty-one years in jail and $46,000 in fines. The eleven-count indictment charged them and other members of the company with "impeding Federal officers in pursuit of their duties," *charges having nothing to do with failure to pay the tax bill.* At no time during the subsequent May trial was the actual issue confronted, and all of the specified infractions had occurred between the official seizure and closing, and the date of the unauthorized performance of *The Brig,* a period of four days in October.

After a much publicized trial in which they acted as their own legal representatives, the Becks were found guilty by the twelve-man jury and on June 5 were sentenced to prison; Julian for sixty days, Judith for thirty. The sentence was postponed to allow them to go with the company to London where *The Brig* was to open, and they were released on bail: Julian $1,000, Judith $500. Much was written about the trial and the circumstances leading up to it; everything has been told and retold. There were many questionable points in the government's testimony, and there is still the possibility that certain legal provisions were ignored which if appealed might have shown the government's action to have been illegal. The case was never appealed to a higher court, but the fact remains that its real issue, nonpayment of the taxes, was never dealt with. As circumstances of the American tour four years later would indicate, it never would, and perhaps never could, be dealt with in any conclusive way.

On September 2, 1964 *The Brig* premiered at London's Mermaid Theatre. This was the Living Theatre's third trip abroad. In the summer of 1961 the first tour had been made to Rome, Turin, Milan, Paris, Berlin and Frankfurt with a repertory that had consisted of *The Connection, Many Loves,* and *In the Jungle of Cities;* the second tour was in April and May of 1962, playing *The Connection, The Apple,* and *In the Jungle of Cities* in Germany, Holland and Belgium as well as in Paris and Zurich. This trip to

London with *The Brig* would be its last "visit" abroad. The enthusiastic response of the London audiences echoed that of the earlier tours, and, encouraged by this, the Living Theatre decided to remain abroad as long as it could.

After London, *Mysteries* would be created in Paris, *The Brig* would be played in Belgium and in Berlin, and in mid-December the Becks would return to America to begin their prison sentences: Julian in Danbury Prison in Connecticut, Judith in the Passaic County Jail in New Jersey. In January and February of 1965, respectively, Judith and Julian would rejoin the company in Europe for a period of time that proved to be a determining influence in the development of the Living Theatre.

At the end of November of that crucial year, 1964, a farm would be lent to them in Heist-sur-Mer, a bleak village on the Belgain coast, where they would live until February of 1965. Poverty, starvation and illness, the ravaging prelude to the European years—it was through the hardships and grimness of Heist that the amazing physical and psychological fortitude developed, and in its aftermath the Living Theatre would be reborn as a total and unique communal entity. As *The Brig* had marked the turning point in its creative style and technique and had influenced its later productions, Heist would leave an indelible imprint on each individual and effect a metaphysical separation between those who had experienced it and those who had joined later on.

Also to come from that period was a production of Genet's *The Maids*, which Judith had directed and Julian had staged by mail from their prison cells in the United States—the

11

company rehearsing and constructing its set in Heist-sur-Mer. *The Maids* would premiere in Berlin on February 26, 1965.

As the company began to expand and as families and children became a part of its permanent community, money was always a problem. Though the cost of supporting itself had increased considerably since the year at Heist, the eager European response eventually made things somewhat easier, and aside from tours and festivals, there were movie and television appearances to keep them going.

The Living Theatre evolved from the earliest experiments as a theatre of poetry through *The Connection,* its first major break with poetic theatre, and *The Brig.* The work created abroad is strikingly different from anything previously done. Its primary impetus was a need for a common language in which to communicate with its audiences as it traveled from country to country across the Continent. A non-verbal dramatic idiom had to be found that would go beyond words and reach the public on a level that transcended the need for language. Through the writings of Artaud and various spiritual and metaphysical doctrines, and through the use of drugs that expanded consciousness, a "magic" was created that eliminated the need for and the barriers established by verbal communication. At present about one-third of its membership is non-American, and all of the actors, American and European, have fluency in at least three languages; it has a thoroughly international mien.

It is impossible to separate the Living Theatre's art from its political ideology, and as its off-stage action became increasingly controversial—either through political activism

12

of individual members, or through the unconventional collective life style—problems would eventually arise in the form of bans and harassments by local officials in certain cities, a prime factor in its decision to live as a rootless, migratory community without a permanent base. Through its skillful combination of art, ideology, and collective existence, it would gain an important position in the revolutionary parallel culture of Europe; in purely sociological and apolitical terms, it would become an influential part of the international Pop phenomemon of the 1960's.

In the European years of traveling and performing, the company would visit every country, playing in cities from Stockholm to Madrid and from Dublin to Belgrade. Four years later it would make a return visit to an America that had absorbed so many of its earlier experiments into its present cultural climate and was now capable of appreciating one of the most vital sources of these influences. It was important to bring them back. But most important, it was necessary that they come back, because there was a new generation, a restless, energetic one whose young people were demanding change and a cultural revolution that aimed to free all men from repressive social systems and put an end to war and violence. And this young generation had never heard of the Living Theatre.

The Living Theatre Company
Directed by Julian Beck and Judith Malina

Jim Anderson
Pamela Badyk
Cal Barber
Julian Beck
Rod Beere
Carol Berger
Odile Bingisser
Mel Clay
Rufus Collins
Pierre Devis
Echnaton
Carl Einhorn
Gene Gordon
Roy Harris
Jenny Hecht
Frank Hoogeboom
Henry Howard
Nona Howard

Steve ben Israel
Alexander van der Linden
Birgit Knabe
Judith Malina
Mary Mary
Michele Mareck
Gianfranco Mantegna
Gunther Pannewitz
Dorothy Shari
William Shari
Luke Theodore
Steve Thompson
Jim Tiroff
Diana van Tosh
Leo Treviglio
Petra Vogt
Karen Weiss
Peter Weiss

At the full moon in July we arrived in Paris and went to an Arab café.
At the full moon in August one of us went mad in London, and Steve
   was hit by a truck while marching in the streets.
At the full moon in September we gathered in a cellar in London and
   spoke for the first time of Frankenstein.
At the full moon in October we were rehearsing the Mysteries in
   Paris.
At the full moon in November we played the Brig in Berlin for
   millions on television.
At the full moon in December I was in jail in New Jersey.
At the full moon in January I visited Julian in jail in Connecticut.
At the full moon in February we played the Mysteries in the Carre
   circus in Amsterdam.
At the full moon in March we played the Brig in Turin.
At the full moon in April we played the Mysteries in Rome.
At the full moon in May we performed the Brig in Naples.
At the full moon in June Garry was sick in Paris.
At the full moon in July we had a Chinese dinner with Elsa Morante
   in Berlin.
At the full moon in August we completed the structure for Franken-
   stein in Berlin.
At the full moon in September we were rehearsing Frankenstein
   desperately in Berlin.
At the full moon in October we returned from Venice to Berlin.
At the full moon in November we played the Maids and Mysteries at
   the Intercontinental in Frankfort.
At the full moon in December we traveled from Malmö to Göteborg.

17

At the full moon in January we arrived in Bologna.
At the full moon in February we played the Mysteries in the Palazzo Durini in Milano twice in a day.
At the full moon in March we traveled from Catania to Siracusa where we saw the Greek Theatre by moonlight.
At the full moon in April we celebrated the Seder in a hotel room in Banja Luka Yugoslavia after performing the Mysteries.
At the full moon in May we played the Brig in Parma.
At the full moon in June we were rehearsing Frankenstein in Reggio Emilia.
At the full moon in July we were returning from the Theatre of Nations in Paris, over the Alps, back to Italy.
At the full moon in August we opened Frankenstein in Cassis in a new production at the sea's edge.
At the full moon in September we played Frankenstein in Berlin.
At the full moon in October we played the Mysteries in Venice and staged the Lachmyian juggernauts for Antigone.
At the full moon in November we played the Mysteries in Amsterdam and rehearsed the entrance of Antigone with Polyneikes.
At the full moon in December we played the Mysteries in Amsterdam and rehearsed the faces of the people for Antigone.
At the full moon in January we staged the prologue for Antigone in Krefeld.
At the full moon in February we played Antigone in Dinslaken.
At the full moon in March we rehearsed the Bacchus Dances in Perugia in the freezing Palazzo.
At the full moon in April Julian flew to Morocco, and we played the Maids at the Palazzo Durini in Milano.
At the full moon in May we played Frankenstein in Naples.
At the full moon in June most of the company traveled to Rome to make a movie.
At the full moon in July I was in the American Hospital in Paris with Isha Manna two days old.
At the full moon in August we walked with Garry in the Latin Quarter and visited the Orangerie in Paris where we were rehearsing Frankenstein.

At the full moon in September we performed the Mysteries in Paris
and moved from Isha's birthplace on the Rue
Troyon.
At the full moon in October we performed Antigone in Brussels.
At the full moon in November we performed Bussotti's opera
"Passion According to de Sade" and quelled a
riot on stage with a sit-in in Bordeaux.
At the full moon in December we performed Antigone in Paris.
At the full moon in January we performed Antigone in Lucerne and
rehearsed a new staging of the messenger scene.
At the full moon in February we were settling into Cefalù, Sicily,
preparing to rehearse Paradise Now.
At the full moon in March we were rehearsing Paradise Now in
Cefalù and Julian made a lecture on John Cage.
At the full moon in April we celebrated the Seder in Cefalù and
rehearsed the Totem Poles for Paradise Now.
At the full moon in May we visited the cathedrals of Tours and
Chartres and arrived in Paris at midnight at the
start of the General Strike.
At the full moon in June we worked on the staging of the Rites for
Paradise in the garden of the Palace of the
Popes in Avignon.
At the full moon in July we held our first rehearsal on the stage of
the Cloister of the Carmelites in Avignon and
read the Texts of the Actions.
At the full moon in August we worked on the Actions for Paradise
in the garden of Voltaire's house in Geneva.
At the full moon in September we were on the M.S. Aurelia en route
to an American tour.
At sea   September 1968[1]

Monday, September 9, 1968

Pier 40, New York City. It is 10:30 A.M. and the Living Theatre has just arrived aboard the *S.S. Aurelia,* having spent ten days on the high seas, or high on the spent seas, depending on one's view of either the Living or marine pollution. The Living Theatre *en masse* is an unbelievable spectacle for any hour of the day, or so it seems at first sight as thirty-some adults of various nationalities and sexes, plus nine babies (even more undeterminable as to sex and country of origin at first glance) wait in the press lounge for Judith Malina and Julian Beck to come through Customs. Decked out in some of the most fantastic costumes this side of Anywhere, their collective appearance leads one to suspect that the world's flea markets have been depleted, and the dreary press lounge has been transformed into a chaotic circus arena.

But in observing the Living, one is always struck by more than mere "appearances." There is a Presence about them, a pronounced, almost formidable Presence that is the essence of mystique. Yet, here, now, moving as they do within this aura of composure and self-contained different-ness, they exude warmth, openness, an unexpected gentleness of manner. Like all who find security in insecurity, they live outside of social conventions that would inhibit personal contact. The adjective "nice" would seem anemic or incongruous in an era of Super-things, but yes, they are nice. If that Presence is in the mind of the observer, it is, nonetheless, a very real collective quality, one which over the next few months would (in most instances) be maintained amidst the thousands of home-grown dissidents encountered along the way. It was a quality that would be dimensioned by its ability to withstand the fatigue and the tedium of the tour ahead. Later on there would be manifest a certain concentricity in which Julian Beck and perhaps a half dozen others were the center that held—intelligent, very together, often beautifully articulate individuals who took care of business and kept things in order; around them would be the majority of the company, those gifted in other areas but equally responsible in their own way, who—sometimes because of language difficulties, sometimes not—weren't so verbally inclined. The outer circle was that relatively small proportion of "dead weight" that seemed to be along for the ride, on an ego trip of its own, and those who had achieved an ersatz "mystical" level that demanded only enough information to be effluviously boring: one suspected that in an earlier life, in some conventional pre-Living phase of development, they had qualified as "dull-normals."

But here at first encounter one notices only the total Presence. And the morning still drags on, having given way over the past couple of hours to a more subdued turmoil as piles of luggage reach mountainous proportions and children become irritable, their ill temper seeming to rise in inverse ratio to the onset of adult fatigue. Waiting, staring, the bitter black coffee

long since drained away, one recalls other "groups" . . . performers, film-makers, Andy Warhol's "superstars," the latter
really more entourage than ensemble. It seemed that in a
given social situation, when any group was the center of attention within a limited area, its members soon attempted to
separate themselves, to compete as individuals for the outsider's attention. But here were thirty-four definitely unique
individuals, similar only in terms of being unusual looking,
engulfed in an undeniable aura of One-ness. The outsider is
immediately aware of this coherence, is perhaps put off by
it since it only heightens his feelings of outside-ness, and
despite their relaxed and friendly attitudes, that Presence
becomes even more overwhelming. The Living's integration
is so complete that at first encounter it is almost impossible
to recognize the Americans from the Europeans. All are
multilingual, and most of the Americans, about two-thirds
of the troupe, seem to have speech patterns and inflections
that show foreign influence. To add to the confusion, the
foreign third speaks English in pretty much the same manner.

It is one-thirty when the Becks, finally cleared through
Customs, appear in the harsh sunlight on the sidewalk outside of the lounge, their arrival setting off a flurry of excitement as those inside rush to greet them. Tears are shed,
kisses given, pictures taken. Judith, tiny, nervous, smiling
through tired tear-glistened eyes, a childlike vulnerability
belying the force and the madness that hold the creative
genius of Judith; Julian, tall and sinewy, stands beside her
holding their baby daughter, the breeze blowing his wavy
gray hair back from an incredible face, imposing in its mes-

23

sianic repose, marvelous in its openness and smiling mobility, a face hewed beneath his smooth bald pate: "The bald man with the long hair," Judith once referred to him jokingly.

And now a burst of activity, the rejuvenation and renewal of chaos, the waiting line of automobiles is loaded with luggage and the Living; the crazy morning is over.

It was about two weeks later, while the Living was performing at Yale on the first leg of its tour, that I realized the enormity of the project I had set for myself. There I was to understand that this book wasn't merely concerned with a "theatrical event." New Haven provided the first opportunity of seeing confrontations between the Living and the desperate forces of law and order, of witnessing encounters . . . some equally hostile but for rational reasons . . . with student activists and resistance leaders, with black militants and ghetto leaders, all of them young revolutionaries trying, like the Living, to create a new society to replace an old one turned in on itself and atrophied by leaders who, in their own self-interest, would protect it from these vital winds of change. For the first time I understood that the Living Theatre was a creative barometer for gauging where this country is at today and where it could easily be tomorrow.

America was new to me, as it was for many of the Living. Raised in it, educated in it, a citizen of it, the America that I had inhabited turned out to be an isolated state of mind, perhaps even a form of psychosis, in which, despite its many faults, a delusion of belonging could be nurtured without raising too many serious doubts. I did not know the America

24

that had voted for Goldwater and was now prepared to vote for Wallace, the America that condones the bloodshed of the Chicago convention or sees righteousness in the assassins of those who might have saved it, the plastic America with the petrified mind, the bed-rock America with the synthetic soul. Nor did I know that bright new America of a young generation which, having participated in its sexual and psychedelic revolutions, were now activists in a political movement, the goals of which, nebulous and naive though they may have sounded at times, did seem more humanitarian than anarchic. I knew that these other Americas existed, but we had never been introduced.

New England, the Midwest, the West Coast, the Southwest; the United States in 1968. The Living Theatre had refused bookings in the South, and having enlisted as a sort of inside-outsider, I was denied the privilege of traveling with them into still another country of America.

Part Two
The American Tour

Monday, September 16:
Yale School of Drama, New Haven

This was the first stop of the Living Theatre's tour and it proved to be extremely successful on many levels, mainly because the enthusiastic reception at Yale provided a much-needed boost for the company's morale, but also because of certain back-stage confrontations during performances of *Paradise Now* which turned a few heads and indicated that the Living Theatre may have been out of the country too long. The most publicized confrontation, of course, was the arrest of the Becks and three members of the company, four Yale students, and a sixteen-year-old boy after the second performance of *Paradise Now*.

But let's go back two weeks to the opening night at Yale. This was the first American opening, probably the most important one of the entire tour because none of the four theatre-pieces had ever been done before in the United States, and secondly, but more significant, because of their political involvements before leaving for Europe, because of the Becks' outspoken contempt for the American system, because of exaggerated press reports concerning the company's participation in the May riots in Paris (only a few members of the company—the Becks, Steve ben Israel,

Gianfranco Mantegna, Jim Anderson, Petra Vogt, and Carl Einhorn had actually been involved), the Avignon riots, drugs, taxes, politics: the fun-house mirror of media distortion. So many "becauses," but really because no one had been told what to think of them yet, there had been a news black-out on their New York arrival. The news media were lying in wait, ready to pounce on them if they made one bad move. This naturally created some tension, but as was later discovered, the Living functions at its peak under stress, and this American premiere was pulled off with such brilliance that, aside from Martin Gottfried's vividly perceptive review of this performance in *Women's Wear Daily,* the tension shifted to the critical camp, which then decided to hold out a couple of weeks until the New York opening at the Brooklyn Academy of Music, definitely a tougher room to work. Where the so-called "Establishment" press was concerned, the Living was to separate the hip from the square all the way down the line. The point is not that it's hip to like the Living Theatre and square not to, but that any reviewer has to be hip enough out front to know that standards of conventional dramatic criticism can't be imposed in this case, and he must be flexible enough to get down with the action, attacking or applauding viscerally, not, for example, with the plodding intellect of Eric Bentley's three-week snit with Clive Barnes in the *New York Times* and *Time* magazine on the Yale opening of *Mysteries and Smaller Pieces:*

What is less admirable . . . and peculiarly ironic . . . about the Beck-Malina troupe is that it is a mirror image of so much that it claims to hate. It hates aggression, but its silences are aggressive. It professes non-violence, but its pieces drip violence. . . . It preaches love, but it

30

would rather rape an audience than woo it. It loathes uniformity and the uniform, yet the cast is drilled to such impersonal military precision that it most resembles a company of Green Berets.

In its usual glib, goosey-fruit, and peculiarly ironic manner *Time* managed to miss a few points, and it was almost inevitable that *Newsweek* would have to straighten things out with competence and intelligence:

In one sense they are beyond criticism . . . exasperating, boring, outrageous, and high-handed as they can be, their authenticity of spirit is beyond question as is their desire to settle for nothing but real change in the human beings who are the ultimate substance of both art and life.

Anyway, back to New Haven for the American premiere, tonight *Mysteries and Smaller Pieces.* Riding up from New York with co-producer Beverly Landau and English movie and theatrical producer Oscar Lewenstein, the man responsible for taking the Living Theatre to England four years ago after their American troubles, we arrive at the Hotel Taft a couple of hours before showtime and learn that the performance is sold out and much excitement is in the air. But then we run into a few members of the company and it is quite apparent that morale isn't what it could be. Some are talking about returning to Europe as soon as possible. Nothing has happened, the rehearsals went well, no "incidents," no busts (yet), no scenes, just general frustration and problems of adjustment. Of course, New Haven isn't the best introduction to the States, but it's still a damnsight better than, say, Selma, Alabama, for a troupe of thirty-four outrageously dressed people with an equal number of head arrangements to unhinge your average American local gentry. Boredom is the prime problem, a startling disclosure in view of the wild reputation that follows the Living where-ever they go.

Don't worry about a thing. Morale will soar after to-night's show. They'll *love* you. Assurance is given more in consolation than in confidence at this point, since only three people in the room, performers excluded, have seen the present company in any of these new pieces. It is obvious that this assurance is based on their appearances at Max's Kansas City and at the round of parties thrown for them in New York.

Mysteries and Smaller Pieces, the oldest of the four productions of this tour, is a good introduction to the current work of the Living Theatre. The first of their productions to have been created in Europe, its first premiere was October 26, 1964 at the American Center for Students and Artists in Paris where the Living Theatre had been invited to give a special presentation. Although less complex than the work which was to follow, *Mysteries* is the bridge between that work and the turning point of *The Brig.* Moreover, it is here that one of the most vital directions of the present repertory is manifest: the highly sensitive "feedback" on which much of the work operates. In a simplistic form this comes across as interaction between audience and performer (or performance), but the Living Theater, deriving its technique in part from Artaudian concept and in equal part from what must be accepted as magic, attempts to take the spectator to such an intense level of emotional involvement that he is forced to react. That reaction, be it a positive or a negative one, becomes in a sense the psychic energizer behind which

32

the company works. In other words, this "feeding back" comes from an interplay of *tensions. Mysteries* holds the comparatively gentle seed of this device, but the later *Paradise Now* is totally dependent upon the conscious control and manipulation of it.

In the months to follow, *Mysteries* and *Paradise Now* sometimes comprised a two-night engagement at a college or university, and on those occasions it usually seemed that, for those seeing the company for the first time, some indispensable links were missing. In seeing *Mysteries,* the oldest piece in the present repertory, juxtaposed with the newest, *Paradise Now,* the direction in which the Living Theatre has been moving over the years becomes apparent . . . indeed obvious . . . in terms of effecting a total liberation from conventional dramatic form. However, one can easily be misled by the seeming lack of structure to these two productions. Without also seeing *Frankenstein* and *Antigone,* the organic style and the full impact of the Living Theatre are severely diminished and that liberation can become meaningless.

Two important encounters occurred at Yale, encounters which were to recur in different forms over the next few months in just about every city where *Paradise Now* was performed. The more publicized confrontation took place on the opening night of that show when the Becks and three members of the company—Jenny Hecht, Nona Howard, and Pierre Devis—were arrested along with five members of the audience (mostly Yale students), one of whom was a sixteen-year-old boy from Weston, Connecticut. *Paradise Now* will be discussed at greater length later on; within the context

33

of this situation it is necessary to know only that shortly after it begins the female performers have stripped down to bikinis (very modest bikinis, at that; their form following function much too closely to arouse what's known as "prurient interest" . . . whatever that means) and the men are in an assortment of G-strings and loincloths (very imaginative constructions with Very High P. I. quotient), and that it ends (or, more correctly, is supposed to end) with the cast leading the audience out into the streets to begin the revolution that will bring Paradise now.

Because of all the pre-arrival publicity about the controversies and conflicts aroused by this show in Avignon where it premiered August '68 amidst student riots and in Geneva where near-riot conditions prevailed during its performances (performances of *Paradise Now* have since been banned in Geneva), the New Haven police had been alerted to expect trouble . . . and when police expect trouble they usually arrange to get it. All week the theatre and backstage entrances had been so accessible to the public that a lot of clothing, money, and other personal possessions had been stolen from the dressing rooms, but on the opening night of *Paradise Now* one discovered that all those faceless little men who had been sitting in the hotel lobby all week, those funny men who seem to live in hotel lobbies all over the world, turned out to be the faceless fuzz, and suddenly there was that presumed traveling-salesman-from-the-sticks, a compulsive newspaper reader, that one (why hadn't he been picked up for loitering? one wondered), hassling everyone for identification at the stage entrance, cluing you in. Yes, there was going to be trouble tonight; the fix was in.

34

But if the Living surrendered to its collective paranoia, it wouldn't be able to get up in the morning, so the show went on and there they were four hours later chanting "The street . . . to the street . . . ," and the audience surged through the building exits, some carrying members of the cast on their shoulders, many stripped down to their underwear, and that sixteen-year-old boy completely nude. To the street where hundreds of students, unable to get into the sold-out performance, awaited the finale in the hope that it would trigger their own protest and begin the violent revolution that they had in mind. The police were waiting, too, lots of them, at the intersection with two paddy wagons stationed behind a barrier of patrol cars.

Conflicting reports emerge. Some say that it was the students carrying the performers who had zealously led them straight into the police cordon, others say that only Julian and Judith were student-borne into the barricade and that the other subsequently arrested members had followed them in support; some insist that the police were waiting to arrest only the Becks, who, it should be remembered, are still on probation after their arrests four years ago. But the undisputed information that came out of it was that there was no violence and all were treated as well as could be expected under such circumstances. Held in custody for almost four hours, each was finally released on $300 bond.

In court the following morning, September 27, the Becks and Pierre Devis faced charges of indecent exposure, Judith, Jenny, and Nona having also been charged with resisting arrest, and October 1, the following Tuesday, was set as the trial date. Under the morals code of the state of Connecticut, those arrested for indecent exposure must undergo an examination for venereal disease before being permitted to stand trial, so with the exception of the peace-breaching, arrest-resisting Nona, clap tests were uppermost on the afternoon's agenda. Meanwhile, Robert Brustein, noted drama critic and dean of the Yale drama department, met with the chief of police and an agreement was reached whereby the two remaining performances (both sold out) of *Paradise Now* could be played without intervention provided the cast did not leave the theatre at the end.

The case was postponed until October 3, the day after their triumphant opening at the Brooklyn Academy of Music, and the five returned to New Haven for the trial. The trial, which included testimonies for the defense by Robert Brustein and cartoonist Jules Feiffer, at Yale for rehearsals of a play, resulted in the acquittal of Julian, Pierre, and Judith on charges of indecent exposure. Judith, however, was fined $100 for "obstructing a police officer." Actually, on the night of the disorders, in seeing Julian being led in his G-string to a paddy wagon, Judith had said to a nearby policeman, "Hey, that's my husband," whereupon the policeman had obligingly escorted her into the vehicle with Julian. Her case, as with that against Jenny Hecht, seemed to rest on a small technicality—in neither case had the arresting officer informed them that they were under arrest. Legally speaking, they had not been formally arrested. Jenny's case was dismissed, those against the students were dismissed, a spectator arrested with them was fined $10, and the case against the minor, "Windy" Simmons of Weston, Connecticut, resulted in his being placed on a year's probation: if he was arrested again for any reason within that period, he would be institutionalized again; if not, the case was closed.

Two weeks later Windy popped up in *Paradise* at the Brooklyn Academy of Music, this time respectably sporting a G-string. His quiet, intelligent manner took on a boyish shyness when he spoke, but one suspected that beneath it all Windy had a mission. Maybe he didn't know it yet and maybe it was all nonsense, but Windy, wiry and sandy haired, didn't seem like an ordinary kid who was running away with a circus. At the hearing after the New Haven bust he had stood calmly before the judge, flanked by his parents and his psychiatrist . . . the mother's face prematurely aged and tense, the lips thin and taut, shoulders slightly hunched with anxiety beneath the Peck and Peckish outfit; the father medium height and stocky, hair grayed and thinned from the pursuit of wealth, thick neck muscles tensed, jutting the jaw and fixing the mouth in a bulldog curl, a mean-looking man who knew Right from Wrong. Windy had listened coolly, unconcerned, as his father explained to the judge that his son was a genius, that his son was unmanageable, that his son had been under psychiatric care, in expensive institutions, for a good many of his sixteen years. If only the judge would try to *understand,* everything would be all right. And later that morning, with composure far beyond his age, Windy had sat in the courtroom alone—for his father, without a glance in his direction, having done his Duty, standing-by-one's-flesh-and-blood, it's called, had strode away and now sat on the opposite side of the room taking care not to look over at his son; his mother, awed by a genius I. Q. and a husband she understood even

37

less, sat behind her son beside the kind-looking psychiatrist (perhaps the only one any of them really cared about or who really cared about the boy), and gave in to an expression of helpless confusion, her once-pretty face softened to undermine a rigidity imposed by living with strangers.

Another stranger, a young woman seated beside Windy, had held out her hand to him and he had clasped it, held on to it tightly and eagerly with eyes steady ahead but glistening, and like so much else in his carefully attended spirit, their tears were held back. Only the firm grip on the hand held out to him gave away the desperation and yearning within that young spirit. When time came for the young woman to leave she withdrew her hand carefully, apologetically, and turning around to his mother, she said, "Don't leave him—he needs you." And the mother replied quietly, "God bless you."

The New Haven Trial: From the Diary of Judith Malina

In the courtroom, one of those cluttered, confused courtrooms in a courthouse not yet modernized and coping with 18th century architecture, not well made over. After long hassling a date for trial is set. Yom Kippur.

Those charged with indecent exposure are breaching one of the laws which fall into the category of the "Chastity Laws" and must take a test for venereal disease. We are dispatched to the Health Department. Here: in a building in the nouveau-fortress style of modern concrete and glass we are greeted by a large sign warning us that this building is protected by dogs. A muse, who complains that we are ruining her weekend by all appearing in a bunch like this, takes blood for our wassermans. "I'm not allowed to take my clothes off without a wasserman."

38

On Friday the 4th we drive to New Haven for the trial. Friends gather: Brustein, Jules Feiffer, and dozen of the students who are "our friends in Hew Haven."

The judge is straight, neither good nor bad: he has a tired look. We saw him last week dispose of a couple of unfortunates with a cool dispatch, if not particularly merciful, he is at least not a wisecracking joker like so many municipal judges who soften the horror of their job for themselves by embittering the poor with their mockery.

Judge Alexander has a reputation as a good guy.

The prosecuting attorney is a pleasant young man who doesn't really have it in for us, but presents his case to win it. Our lawyer is nervous, but well prepared and full of energy. He has with him a smart lady lawyer named C..... R?, who whispers to him during the trial but says very little herself, except once when she suggests that the whole thing be dropped. Jenny and Jill and Nona are dismissed because the arresting officer could not identify them. John Laporta, a Yale student, and Bruce, the English director are dismissed.

Officer Sullivan is a young man who has been on the police force for fourteen months and has already made over 300 arrests according to his testimony. Is that more than an arrest a day? He's nervous at first, but after a while he answers less formally. The big question seems to be whether or not Julian or Pierre were "exposed."

At first the officer says that my breasts were exposed, later that it was only my left breast, and then later that it was only accidental, and that charge is dropped . . . Sullivan claims that he saw Pierre and Julian's genitals, and our witnesses will describe the costumes of *Paradise* to refute this . . .

As for Ira and I, we are charged with interfering with an officer, and Sullivan describes how we "wedged" ourselves between him and the paddy-wagon to prevent Julian's arrest.

Bob Brustein and Jules Feiffer testify as to what they saw. A student named Philip Welch testifies as to what he saw. Julian is religious and sombre on the stand, even when asked ridiculous questions about his awareness of his genitals: he maintains a cool superior air. I try to be so direct and open that no one will disbelieve me, not that

I have faith it will work but I'd rather be straight. Ira Cohen fakes and to me and Julian it's plain and we regret it. Pierre can't understand the legal jargon and answers questions simply in his lace cossack and they think he's too dumb to cross examine.

Finally, after a day of wasteful procedures the judge, so as not to let us off completely drops all the exposure charges and holds Ira and me for interfering with an officer, and fines us with $100 each. We appeal because of my probation.[1]

The courtroom is lined with Yale students and a few professors, Werner Roder, Bob Brustein, Arnold Weinstein, Jules Feiffer who happens to be in New Haven for the opening of his first play . . . on the stand he identifies himself as "cartoonist and playwright," Gordon Rogoff.

This assemblage of intellectuals watches the "due process" with greater than usual interest, for it is the time of The Choosing of the Sides, and the validity of the court of law as an arena of action is on everybody's mind. And the "riots" that the police provoke among peaceful demonstrators, as opposed to scenes in which the police are provoked is a burning question, especially to those who were not in Chicago, at the barricades, or in the scenes of action. It's useful for them, as they see the lies win over the truth, to re-evaluate their meaning of law and order. Brustein had publicly criticized our behaviour in the Federal Court at the time of the Living Theatre Trial; now he saw how the sense of outrage is hard to control, himself angered at misconstruction of reality by the process of lie . . . and upheld.

It's useful for the hundreds of students who saw me walk peacefully into the wagon at the policeman's irritation That's my husband, may I go with him . . . gesture of assent Entry to hear the story constructed differently into a fiction about resisting police; to me fined and found guilty, to learn that the lie of the policeman always wins over plain spoken truth in the court of law.

It's good, too, that this can be demonstrated in a small, safe and unimportant case where there's no real suffering, but where the

[1]The Becks are both in the last year of a five-year period of probation following their release from prison in 1965.

suffering of the thousands in the jails, in the deathhouses, in front of the firing squads is emblematically carried on with all this shrieking horror under the banner of "In God We Trust."

Everywhere, bit by bit, swifter and slowly, the shame of the old values is exposed.

In the time of the chosing of the sides only the totally blind can turn away from the light.

It's shining in our eyes. Makes us blind. Light of Liberty. But in her sinister hands she holds the book of laws, no one uses the word Liberty. It is a notion fit to revive.

It's useful, even without knowing it to set an example.

J. Feiffer says to me, leaning over the lawyer's desk, "Can't they see in his face [the cop's] that he's lying?" No they can't . . . Yes, they can, but they won't because they are defending something else. . . . Because somehow you just can't let people "get away with such things."

Only the caricaturist, who is expert at drawing the lying face, the false look, he can see it.

Racing back to Brooklyn for the *Frankenstein* performance.

The second confrontation, less publicized but more important in terms of the Living's "orientation" to the United States in 1968, took place backstage during the second performance of *Paradise Now*. This was their initial confrontation with radical young dissidents, and as was often to be the case all across the country, this one began with disturbing hostility; unlike so many that were to follow, this one was also disturbingly enlightening . . . enlightening not because one was being apprised of something new, but because of that sudden, horrible awareness that comes from knowing all too well and having *done* nothing—for one hundred and three years.

As students in the theatre goaded and taunted the actors, fed on them and brought the action to a dangerous peak in their attempt to use the Living Theatre as a trigger for their own frustrations, the important confrontations were taking place in a small lounge just off the stage entrance where members of the SDS paid visits, where a group of Guevara supporters came, where the most radical black militants from New Haven's ghetto, members of the Hill Parents Association, came, all with disdain and animosity, to challenge the Living Theatre, to put its members down for being out of touch and not knowing where the revolution was at in this Country. The most severe and articulate condemnations came from the black militants and their spokesman Ronnie Johnson, who like the Becks was also on probation and who, paradoxically, was busted on returning home to the Hill ghetto later that night.

"That non-violent shit died when King was shot, Jim. We ain't talking non-violence anymore. . . . You cats better get your shit together and find out what's happening here . . . Now!"

Seated in an armchair, Ronnie Johnson, heavy-set and bearded with eyes hidden behind dark glasses, was an impressive speaker, his contemptuous criticism coming across with the utmost cool. More of the cast drifted backstage to argue with him, to try to convince him that non-violence was still possible, but Johnson wasn't having any.

"Where are you dudes going next?" he asked.

"Brooklyn Academy of Music," someone told him.

"Listen, you lay that shit down in Brooklyn and some of those Bedford-Stuyvesant cats'll bust your heads open. They ain't going to listen to that."

Meanwhile, a few feet away bedlam was breaking loose in the theatre as the audience unleashed an assault, demanding that the doors be opened, that either those outside be allowed in or that the Living lead those inside into the street. Unwilling . . . possibly even unable; this was only about the eighth performance of *Paradise Now* . . . to handle the attack on the students' terms, the Living had tried to

44

convince them that such action would be self-defeating because the police were surrounding the building and waiting for just such an action, and in an effort to restore order and get things under control, they had begun the next action of the play. Out front the pandemonium had subsided, but backstage the outrage was just cresting as the radicals put the Living down in no uncertain terms for copping out and not having dealt with the situation. It was finally agreed that the Living and Johnson's contingent would get together when neither would be interrupted by a performance, and a time was set for the following Sunday afternoon.

On Sunday afternoon Johnson and two other black militants met with about twenty members of the Living Theatre in a rehearsal hall beneath the theatre. The mood was less belligerent now, the opposing camps seeming to have developed a mutual respect for each other's methods. Johnson had realized that despite their nonviolent approach and four years abroad—the Living had taken an active part in the May riots in Paris where they had helped to bring about the occupation of the Odeon, the Avignon riots last summer—the Living was definitely into what was happening, perhaps even a little ahead of it. On their part, the members of the Living were very much tuned in to Johnson's criticism and accusations, for this was their first direct confrontation with America Today . . . perhaps they *had* been away too long. Those who had taken part in the Paris riots knew that despite Julian's fervid defense of non-violence, such tactics might not be possible until a violent revolution was effected, sooner (than it was comfortable to contemplate) or later (much

45

later, than it should have been), between the old and the new Americas. Johnson spoke with less vehemence today, but none of the passionate determination was missing:

"You dudes were great five years ago with that nonviolence, but you've got to change up now. This is a war and there's no room for nonviolence in war. In that play you created a situation and then you didn't deal with it. You didn't let the people deal with it either. You went back to the script, like a Broadway play. You can't expect people to swallow it and then tell them to vomit it up. All you're doing then is perpetuating yourselves. If you create that situation, you've got to leave it out there.

"You guys say you're for the revolution, you're anarchists, but you stay inside the proscenium arch. You can't deal from there. This is the United States of motherfucking America, and when you talk about revolution in this country you're talking about taking The Man's shit away from him . . . shooting him with his own shit. There's no room for individualism anymore; you've got to stop thinking like thirty different people and direct yourselves under one mind. That's where it's at now. There's no more individualism. Later, maybe, but now you've got to get your shit together. The Man's got his shit together, that's why he's so strong. Get yours together, Jim, 'cause where it's at is bloody revolution."

Mysteries and Smaller Pieces

The house-lights go off (as in all of the pieces, the proscenium curtain is never used) and a spotlight shines on an actor who stands, stage front and center, absolutely motionless, head lifted proudly and staring directly into the audience, chest jutting forward, hands on hips with elbows thrust backward, the feet planted firmly together. It is a static, yet somehow aggressive, position miraculously maintained throughout this opening segment of *Mysteries*. There is no apparent reason, no "meaning" for his being there, but by "doing" nothing at all while demanding their complete concentration, his presence gradually intimidates and incites the audience, arousing it to a pitch where ultimately he becomes a "target," a motionless, expressionless, and silent butt for the unsettled spectators' hostility. . . . "Is this the *living* theatre?" "Louder . . . we can't hear you!" "We paid to be entertained." And so it mounts from humorous insult to anger. Others have joined in, countering with a barrage of insult aimed at the insulters—"Go home and watch television!" "You can't expect pigs to concentrate!" No longer a target, the man frozen in the spotlight is now the trigger for the cross-fire.

47

Suddenly running footsteps are heard from the rear of the auditorium. Loud, heavy footsteps, and actors run down the aisles, arms bent with fists pressed to their chests. It is a servile, thudding gait directed and propelled by some invisible Force, some unspoken Order. They run onstage, up and down the aisles, the theatre reverberates with their clatter, the house-lights go up, and other members of the cast, positioned around the theatre, begin a discordant incantation of everything printed on a one-dollar bill. The movements of the pacing actors now become the mechanical, programmed gestures of labor; digging, carrying, working machinery, they move through the aisles, into the audience, the incantation drones on; the first actor, still fixed onstage and oblivious of the frenetic activity around him, is joined by a second man on stage right in a pose of military rigidity, his arms moving in stiff patterns to accept the invisible objects thrust at him by the runners, all onstage at this point and relentlessly executing an elementary drill exercise with an intensity and focus far beyond its requirements. They fall into military formation, diligently marching, feet stomping, arms swinging in unison . . . forward, back, forward, back, forward once more, they sound off in a gut-roar, One . . . Two . . . Three . . . Four, marking time in place. Someone shouts "Company, HALT!" and instantly they snap to attention. Silence. The second actor in military stance on the opposite side of the stage (the first actor is still unmoved from his original position front and center) takes a step forward and, cloaked in pomposity, bellows out a string of commands in double-talk, to which the men in formation respond with a booming "YES, SIR!" Blackout.

From somewhere in the darkened auditorium a female

voice begins to improvise a song based on Sanskrit words to a guitar accompaniment. The audience settles back and relaxes attentively . . . yes, they are going to be entertained. But, lovely at first, the voice and the music flow on . . . and on, and on. Is she putting us on again? A few snickers then laughter, a flickering of renewed hostility in the remarks. Eventually there comes a muffled sound of movement from the stage and tiny pinpoints of light can be seen, tiny patches of dots that keep multiplying. The lights rise slowly to illumine the entire cast, massed across the stage, slowly moving forward, faces expressionless, arms outstretched with sticks of burning incense clasped between fingers.

There is something ominous in their measured approach, but their faces tell us nothing. Smoke rises from the incense and its pungent odor drifts across the proscenium, the actors move into the theatre, up the aisles, slowly past the awed spectators. Some actors offer spectators sticks of their incense, other spectators begin to reach out and take incense, its heady aroma lingering long after the actors have passed up the aisles. And now ahead of us, Julian Beck sits cross-legged in the center of the bare stage and announces "*Street Songs* by Jackson MacLow." In a clear and carefully modulated voice he intones:

"Stop the War" . . . "Freedom Now" . . . "Change the World" . . . "Free the blacks" . . . "End the draft" . . . and so on, each slogan repeated over and over until the audience begins to join in, and finally it becomes a collective voice, chanting for change, peace. The actors move toward the stage. They are followed by members of the audience, a few timid ones at first, but then more go up, the stage fills, a huge circle is formed then smaller concentric rings evolve,

49

absorbing all the participants who stand with arms about each other's waists and shoulders, swaying gently from side to side; "The Chord," a mystical communal hum, rising and filling the theatre with the intense vibration of spiritual love, like an act of purification that purges and leaves those who experience it comforted and at peace with themselves.

Fifteen, twenty minutes . . . the resonant hum ends, and gradually, grudgingly, those on stage return to their seats, leaving several performers on a stage now brightly lit. A few minutes of yoga breathing exercises ensue before these men and women stand and walk casually from the stage.

The second part of *Mysteries* is comprised of a series of very amusing, split-second *tableaux vivants* and "Lee's Piece," an improvisational sound-movement "game," an actors' exercise, originally conceived for the company by Lee Worley as an attempt to create a language of physical reality in which seven performers . . . in a state of communal understanding, on the same energy level . . . communicate through the exchange of gesture and sound. But the highlight is the final piece, based on Artaud's *The Plague*, in which the cast begins with a progressive re-creation of physical deterioration and madness that is truly horrifying. This piece is so disturbing and so convincing in its impact that as the actors, writhing, wailing, contorted into hideous images of sickness and death, hurl themselves at the audience, people rush forward to help them, cradling them in their arms, lowering them into seats, crying "Help him! Help him!" I have seen their involvement at such a pitch that the tension in the air could almost be touched.

Bodies lie scattered in the aisles as the wailing subsides;

50

shoes have been collected and aligned on stage, reminding us that this tortured animal once walked erect. Six men move forward, the pallbearers who must begin the morbid ritual of burying the dead. One by one the rigid "corpses" are collected, the grueling task is carried out until a pile of bodies is constructed. The men stand in mournful resignation before the fate of all men. Darkness slowly descends on this horrifying vision of earthly hell.

Footnote on "The Chord"

The idea for "The Chord" was borrowed from Joseph Chaikin[1] who had developed it as an exercise. From this exercise the Living Theatre created "The Chord" to express the beauty of collective harmony and spiritual communion. European audiences found it beautiful and very moving *to watch;* the only participants outside of the company itself were friends brought into the circle by members of the company. The spontaneous participation of the audience began in the United States . . . from that opening night in New Haven until the end of the tour . . . and "The Chord" took on another meaning for American audiences. It took on a political and moral significance, and for the young people who came up from the audience "The Chord" became an affirmation, an extraordinary declaration of unity.

[1]Joseph Chaikin is the founder and director of the Open Theatre in New York (*America Hurrah!* and *Viet Rock*). Prior to launching his own experimental company in 1963, he was a member of the Living Theatre.

51

Isha Manna

Isha Manna. Isha Manna, infant witch, enormous dark
saucer-eyes stare into you from the startling face of a
very hip cherub. Dark wisps of silky baby-hair, the ends
comma-ed like angel wings, tiny gold earrings on tiny lobes,
a white gown with gold and purple embroidery, Isha Manna
at fourteen months leans toward me from the enfolding arms
of her father, she smiles with a small moist fist pressed to
her mouth, and then letting the little fist drop into the folds
of her dress, she juts that incredible child-face closer to me.
The mouth is opened wide, a fragile birdlike cavern, seemingly toothless, but moistened with teething-drool. But Isha
Manna carries off the whole effect with truly ladylike del-
icacy. Bringing my face to hers, I kiss her moon-check,
warm and flushed with excitement after a busy day with her
parents, Judith Malina and Julian Beck.

But as I kiss her cheek, Isha Manna emits a fretful cry.
I pull away, somewhat taken aback by this reaction, but
then she offers me what appears to be a second chance; the
witchy cherub face is once again pushed toward me, the little
toothless cavern once again proffered.

"What did I do wrong?" I ask Julian.

"She means for you to kiss her on the *mouth*," he laughs. "She knows that's a real kiss."

"Julian, your daughter's a witch."

Julian's face, gaunt, ascetic, inscrutably introspective at times, can move through rapid, almost imperceptible, changes and suddenly burst open, as it does now, radiant with earthy, sensual warmth.

"Yes, I know. She makes me crazy." He holds her closer to him, the small body almost disappearing in his long arms, the amazing face with its mischievous smile burying itself against his shoulder. You can tell that this is just openers for Isha Manna.

Wednesday, October 2: Brooklyn Academy of Music, Brooklyn, (and, even better,) New York

Three weeks in New York City. At the Brooklyn Academy of Music, anyway. Close enough.

The shows go well, reviews generally good-to-rave, and a veritable psoriasis of articles on the Living Theatre everywhere . . . an average of three-a-week in the *Village Voice,* a "rejection" of the Living Theatre by Eric Bentley in the Sunday *New York Times* prompting a less pompous but equally irrelevant "acceptance" by Clive Barnes in the same paper the next week. The co-producer charged with booking the tour and assuring deans at women's colleges that the men in the company wouldn't violate the enrollment ("Just a short lecture-demonstration will do. . . . I don't think they should be on campus too long": lady dean at one of the Seven Sisters) estimated that it would have cost a million dollars if all the publicity received had to be paid for.

A two-part program is videotaped for CBS-TV's *Camera Three;* the first segment, an interview with the Becks hosted by *Newsweek's* Jack Kroll, will be nationally televised on January 12; the second, the Brig Dollar and the Plague from *Mysteries,* on January 19. At the end of the tour it would be learned that the program, particularly its second part,

55

had not passed unnoticed in certain areas of the country—Youngstown, Cleveland, etc., even New York where Norman Vincent Peale had been outraged by what he had *heard* about it. *Camera Three's* director Merrill Brockway exhibits the bulging file, dozens of letters from citizens incensed by what they had viewed (or partially viewed, since many admitted to having tuned in late and not knowing what it was all about) and by those infuriated by what had been *told* them by the merely incensed. There is nothing as durable as America's moral fiber, no feeling as liberated as its moral indignation.

Meanwhile back at the BAM, groupies threaten to become a fire hazard. Dressing rooms are clogged with been-around-teeny-ladies who know Pop sex status when they see it. Those who don't score here can still catch the last show at the Fillmore East. If they can get back to the city in time. Efficiency isn't one of the Living's strong points, and even Avedon had had to wait an hour to photograph them for a proposed exhibition of his work at the Museum of Modern Art.

Filming of a documentary for an educational television channel, begun in Avignon and continued through New Haven, is in the process of being finished during the Brooklyn-New York run when a second film-maker expresses an interest in making a feature-length documentary of the entire tour; someone else wants to make a film version of *Paradise Now,* and yet another party wants to film *Frankenstein.* For all the interest and excitement they may have generated, little of concrete value was to materialize from any of these

56

projects when the tour ended, but here at the outset it seemed a matter of sifting out the best, and other television and film proposals were rejected outright by the Becks.

One can only presume that most of this attention is well intentioned and sincere on whatever level it's dealt from; only the motives could be held suspect-by-association if one cared to take a negative overview of the situation. For in one way or another, whether adamantly for, or vehemently against, the Living Theatre, the mass media were making frantic reparations for the initial news blackout on the September 9 arrival of The Event, and having missed the boat by several weeks, they were now covering it in a desperate effort to show that they were there all along. The gamut is run from serious, perceptive evaluation and ponderous intellectualizing to a flippancy that served only to expose a total lack of comprehension or a mental ossification, either one of which would be considered unforgivable in any other profession. They appeared to be flying up their own assholes in search of a "scoop," an "angle," on a subject that had been "avant-garde" for eighteen years. The paradox was that having returned with a political temper even more outspoken and radical than that which initially had led to its consignment to leperdom, the Living Theatre today is politically and philosophically more controversial than ever before, more theatrically, artistically influential than ever before; in other words, it is more relevant to the present. Relevancy is the key point and it must be viewed from two sides: from mainstream culture, which could now absorb the art of the Living Theatre, and from the advanced sub-

57

culture, which later developments would show to be far more radicalized than the company and rapidly moving beyond its pacifistic ideology. However, it was quite conceivable that the mainstream media could inadvertently succeed in making the Living Theatre *fashionable*.[1]

Still in the process of getting oriented or, in the case of the Americans in the company, re-oriented to what appeared to be America . . . in a couple of weeks they would discover that New York City wasn't America . . . the Living were somewhat removed from the fanfare accorded them. They were accustomed to public controversy and publicity; Europe hadn't exactly ignored them. They had been in films and on television; extensive articles and criticism had been written about them, there were books about them in French and in German; they had been banned, busted, and berated before, and there was reported to be an Interpol file on their activities. None of this was new to them—there was just more of it in New York, and it would take a while to adjust to the magnified scale on which America graded and degraded her Events. Appreciative of the good things written and said about them, untouched by the negative and the flippant (by now nothing more than tired cliché to them) but ultimately dismissing it all with a peculiar blend of sophistication and naïveté, the Living still managed to maintain that communal closeness that was the root of their creative strength. In a sense, they were still vacuum-sealed and immunized for safe

[1]A mini-backlash appeared in the December *Vogue* in the form of a brief editorial goose which dismissed the Living Theatre as "physically unattractive, strident." It had taken the editors months to come up with that scoop. Shows how long "People Had Been Talking About . . ." them.

travel in the overlapping aboveground-underground milieus of New York. But could that protection last, and how long would they be able to withstand the more dangerous social disorders afflicting the rest of the country?

Frankenstein

"The people whom you see seated on the stage are engaged in a meditation, the purpose of which is to lead to the levitation of the person seated in the center."

The dispassionate, measured Voice repeats this in French, Spanish,[1] German. Silence. The meditation continues. Time passes. The multilingual announcement is made again. Silence. The meditation goes on; the group seated in yoga positions facing the audience does not alter its focus. If the meditation succeeds, the play is consummated; if it fails, it becomes a victimization. In time the Voice announces the final phase of the meditation: three minutes of yoga breathing to heal, after which the girl should levitate. The countdown begins . . . three minutes . . . deux minutes . . . un minuto-diente-segundos . . . ein-minute . . . twenty Sekunden . . . dix secondes . . . five seconds . . . *zéro.* . . .

She has failed to levitate. They turn and look at her menacingly . . . they rise in ominous encirclement . . . she is perplexed, she cries out . . . they approach, she tries to es-

[1]In Europe, Italian is used for the lines read in Spanish.

61

cape from the circle, it is useless . . . the net is thrown, the coffin brought. She is forced into it. Her screams are heard as the coffin is nailed shut. The victimization has begun.

The "Skeleton Key" for FRANKENSTEIN

The "skeleton key," or *The Frankenstein Poem,* written by Julian Beck, is the foundation of the play and is used in its program synopses. Since writing it in 1965 in Velletri, Italy, Julian has revised it three times, the currently used version being the Venice synopsis. All three versions of the *Frankenstein Poem* appear in *City Lights Journal,* Number Three; City Lights Books, San Francisco.

THE ACTION   ACT I

A meditation the purpose of which is to lead to levitation
If it succeeds the play is consummated
It it fails it becomes a victimizator
The net is thrown, the coffin is brought
Someone says No
A Procession begins
Others say No
They are hunted, they are electrocuted, they are gassed, they are
    guillotined, they are racked, they are hanged, they are garrotted,
    they are beheaded, they are crucified, they are shot
They plead for their lives
Two survive
A storm rises
Dr. Frankenstein takes the heart of The Victim
The Dead Shall be Raised
Burial by Church and State
They lower the Hanged Man
The Body is Painted
The Workers scream

62

The Old and the Poor come with snow and hammer
How can we end human suffering
The Capitalist speaks   The Marxists march   The Oracle prophesies
The Body reversed
The Generals, the Capitalist, the Marxists, the Workers, and the
    explanatory Voice speak of Automation
The laboratory is constructed
The Cabbalists build the Golem
The Doctor implants the Victim's heart in the Body on the laboratory
    table
Foot brain and eye are grafted
The failure of the heart
Paracelsus appears and directs the graft of the third eye
Freud appears and orders the sexual graft
Norbert Wiener appears and advises the use of electrodes
The electrodes are attached
The Creature moves

THE ACTION   ACT II

Inside the Creature's Head
He Opens his eye
He sees light
He functions
He experiences Miracles and Wonders as his capacities rouse
He sleeps
He dreams of the sea
Shipwreck   Drowning
The brine bubbles up
He wakes
The control Booth instructs him
Educational input   He learns of the world
He translates into the mythological theatre of prototype
Daedalus discovers how to fly   Icarus is launched   Europa is raped
    Pasiphae seduces the bull   The Minotaur is born   The maze is
    made   The Young Men are sacrificed   Theseus kills the
    Minotaur   Icarus falls
He is instructed in the qualities   The Control Booth illustrates

63

He translates into the legend of the enlightenment
Instruction persists
The sail persists
The Four Horsemen of the Apocalypse are riding
The Functions of the Head slash the Ego out into the world
The Body Vanishes
The Word is born
The Creature narrates his story
The Earth People flee
The Creature encounters Death
The Four Horsemen of the Apocalypse are riding
The Functions slash each other out into the world
The Police   The Siren   The Killing
He takes over authority
Authorities take over

THE ACTION   ACT III

The Posse is searching
They say Yes
The Prisoners are fingerprinted, dressed and photographed
World Action
Arrests
World Action
The Whistle Blows
World Action
They move from cell to cell
World Action
The Doctor is arrested
World Action
A note is passed
World Action
The Prisoners eat
A knife is passed
World Action
The Prisoners sleep
The Jailbreak

The Fire   Alarm   Death by Fire
The Creature counts
Man lives

In September, 1965, in Venice, the Living Theatre premiered a production entitled *Frankenstein*. It was said to
have been six hours long. At the Festival of Cassis, summer
of 1966, a second version of *Frankenstein* opened, which
was almost five hours in length. In October of 1967 still a
third version of *Frankenstein* premiered at Dublin's Olympia
Theatre. The last is the only *Frankenstein* of concern here,
and although considerably shorter than the first two, brevity,
or lack thereof, is irrelevant, the difference between each
version unimportant. The fact is that from an almost ob-
sessive attention to detail and structure, persistent changing
and reworking, has emerged a work of absolute creative
genius. As *The Brig* marked the turning point in the Living
Theatre's work, *Frankenstein* is the pinnacle at which all
of its dynamics converge.

In the years since its initial premiere, many writers have
tried to verbalize the visual trip of *Frankenstein*. Victimization being one of the main themes of the play itself,
they in turn have fallen victim to the challenge of attempting
to describe the visual impact of the skeletal structure of its
three-ton, three-tiered set, the various actions taking place
simultaneously within and outside of its fifteen compart-
ments, and who-says-what-to-whom-when. It always makes
for tedious reading (and a tedious writing process, as well)
when this is achieved with any sort of systematic accuracy.
Those who haven't seen it can't possibly imagine what it's all

65

about; those who have seen it have taken a sensual trip and experienced a dramatic totality too visceral to be "victimized" by the limitations of literal delineation. Photographs seldom do it justice, either, because only segments of the structure can be contained within the lens. In order to show the entire set, it is necessary to stand in the rear of the darkened theatre from which the view is invariably obstructed by architectural impediments of the theatre itself; angleshots from the sides distort the structure. Conclusion: *Frankenstein* must be seen live.

Based on the Mary Shelley novel, *Frankenstein* is a collage of Pop art, mytho-science-fiction and the Late Late Show, all of it buttressed by political dogma and moral polemic. It is essentially naïve and corny in plot concept, yet it is so theatrically spectacular, so brilliantly mounted and performed[2] that a kinetic tension is produced, an existing force that is truly electrical. *Frankenstein* is about energy— the animal energy in the human form, the spiritual energy that transcends that form, soul-energy that generates the Possibilities. It is the closest embodiment of Artaud's Theatre of Cruelty that has been attempted in theatre, its impact going so far beyond other attempts (*Marat-Sade,* of course, being the first example that comes to mind) that in retrospect they seem just that—"attempts." *Frankenstein* stands not only as the masterwork of the Living Theatre, but as an artistic masterpiece which happens to take place in the theatre. It is a virtuoso achievement that will never be duplicated by others.

[2]Program credit for direction is given to Julian Beck, but inasmuch as each actor has created his own part in most of the sequences, this is the most collectively created play in the repertory, more so than *Paradise Now,* which, formally speaking, is not a "play."

66

The meditation functions as a prelude to the play. In terms of conventional theatre and for lack of a better word, it is the "overture" that establishes the mood, the tensions —to refer back to the feedback process mentioned in *Mysteries and Smaller Pieces*. The tensions here are created through a dynamic psychic pull: all concentration must be directed toward levitating the girl seated in the center of the stage. But the spectators are still filing into the theatre and those already seated are distracted by the movement of the others, they are whispering and shifting around; synthesis with this scattered psychic force is impossible. Therefore, those involved in the meditation onstage draw from this conflict of energies, using this vast source of unfocused concentration and motion as a reagent for their collective purpose—the levitation. When the movement of the spectators becomes too diffuse the Voice brings it back, rechannels these energies to recharge the energy-focus of those on stage. On another level, the Voice implies through its multilingual pronouncements that even in meditation man is not alone; through automation his most abstracted functions are broadcast to the world.

The countdown is either the end or the beginning of the play, for if the levitation, which must occur on the count of zero, does succeed, the play is completed: if it does not take place, zero is the end—the void from which Frankenstein (played by Julian Beck) will begin the creation of the new world he envisions.

"How can we end human suffering?" His anguished plea, repeated over and over, springs from a sincere determination to elevate the level of human existence and free it from the omnipresence of its injustice and violence. But motivated

67

more by intellect than by compassion, he imparts to his
Creature the mythology and wisdom of the ages, the foundations of modern civilization which man has already succeeded in turning against himself. There is a convolution of
sensibility, and as these ideologies, once conceived in purity,
too, are played out on the three stages of the structure, it
becomes apparent that Frankenstein's noble and worthy
intentions will be corrupted, that involuntarily he will ultimately precipitate evil. His Creation is based on death; in
refusing to accept the wretchedness of the existing human
condition, he is unable to perceive an alternative salvation
in life. Frankenstein is, in a sense, naïve, and this is his flaw.
The sacrificial theme of the levitation is analogized: in fail-
ing to "levitate" the living, the net must be cast again. The
System will cast it now. He will be victimized and tyranny
will continue.

The creation of the New Man becomes a government
project "headed by Doctor Victor Frankenstein," an authoritative Voice announces, the input to the Creature's
head becoming more frantic, myths and legends giving way
to Structure's information, until finally the Ego awakens and
the Creature, childlike and pure in his physical grotesque-
ness, is tossed into the world.

The Creature's Monologue[3]

It is with considerable difficulty that I remember the original era of
my being: all the events of that period appear confused and indis-
tinct. I saw, felt, heard, and smelt, at the same time. By degrees, I

[3]The Creature's Monologue is taken directly from the Mary Shelley
novel and is spoken only in English.

remember, a stronger light pressed upon my nerves, so that I was obliged to shut my eyes. Darkness then came over me, and troubled me; but hardly had I felt this, when, by opening my eyes, the light poured in upon me again. I walked. Before, dark and opaque bodies had surrounded me, impervious to my touch or sight; but I now found that I could wander on at liberty, with no obstacles which I could not either surmount or avoid. The light became more and more oppressive to me; and, the heat wearying me as I walked, I sought a place where I could receive shade. It was dark when I awoke; I felt cold also and half-frightened. I was a poor, helpless, miserable wretch; I knew, and could distinguish, nothing; but feeling pain invade me on all sides, I sat down and wept. Soon a gentle light stole over the heavens and gave me a sensation of pleasure. I started up and beheld a radiant form rise from among the trees. I gazed with a kind of wonder. I felt light and hunger, and thirst, and darkness; innumerable sounds rang in my ears, and on all sides various scents saluted me: the only object that I could distinguish was the bright moon, and I fixed my eyes on that with pleasure. I found a fire which had been left by some wandering beggars and was overcome with delight at the warmth I experienced from it. In my joy I thrust my hand into the live embers, but quickly drew it out again with a cry of pain. How strange, I thought, that the same cause should produce such opposite effects! I arrived at a village. How miraculous did this appear! The huts, the cottages, and houses engaged my admiration. The vegetables in the gardens, the milk and cheese that I saw placed at the windows allured my appetite. I entered one of the cottages; but I hardly placed my foot within the door, before the children shrieked, the whole village was aroused; some fled, some attacked me, until, grievously bruised by stones and many other kinds of missile weapons, I escaped. I obtained a knowledge of the manners, governments, and religions of the different nations of the earth. Was man, at once so powerful, so virtuous and magnificent, yet so vicious and base? To be a great and virtuous man appeared the highest honour than can befall a sensitive being; to be vicious and base appeared the lowest degradation. I could not conceive how one man could go forth to murder his fellow, or even why there were laws and governments; but when I heard details of vice and bloodshed, my wonder ceased, and I turned away with disgust and loathing. The strange system of human society was explained to me. I heard of the division of property, of immense wealth and squalid poverty; of rank, descent, and noble blood. And what was I? Of my creation and creator I was absolutely ignorant; but I knew that I possessed no money, no friends, no kind of property. I was, besides, endued with a figure hideously deformed and loathsome. Was I then a monster, a blot upon the earth, from which all men fled, and whom all men disowned? I learned that there was but one means to overcome the sensation of pain, and that was death. . . .

The Creature, played either by Steve ben Israel or by Henry Howard, begins his monologue in a spotlighted upstage position, and in the course of it, he moves into the audience, back onto the stage and through the structure. The actors in the structure go through the actions he narrates and they repeat his words in unison, following the inflection and the rhythm set by him: the dramatic effect of this choral device creates a sense of quandary and delayed mental reflex—the primitive mind making the passage from its awakening to an external and alien world where he is mistreated and humiliated because of his difference. The inherent goodness of Frankenstein and the knowledge he imparts to the Creature's intellect are meaningless; society has debased and corrupted the Creature into its own image, and, created through an imitative process, he is susceptible to evil influences as well as good ones. He commits murder and a new tyranny is born.

Act III opens with The Search and the structure is now the prison: the audience is being combed for the victims. They are found and interrogated on the way to their imprisonment: "Your name——? Yes. Ever been to——? Yes. You a friend of——? Yes." Everything is known about them, nothing can be refuted; a denial would constitute perjury in the name of survival, and we have come this far by perjuring our souls. Their *Yes* is the charge. "You're under arrest." And executioners become victims: the prison must be filled, for vacancy is a sin on the economy, a social affront to the System!

The prison is not only the symbol of the oppression of the state and of man's repression of man; it is our isolation from one another, the alienation of the spirit when the only communication is in madness.

Frankenstein protests, but to no avail. He, too, is imprisoned; physically by his captors, and spiritually by his guilt for the monster he has naïvely set in motion and the new destruction unleashed by his creation. But guilt is the standard, the currency of a social structure turned in on itself. It is regenerative, self-perpetuating, and yet it is caused by the perversion of innocence. The problem and the solution are the same: The restoration of mankind to his primal innocence, to start again.

"Turn the Creature on!" The stage is back-lit, the structure of the skeletal set towering against the pale backdrop. Edging slowly across the structure, the bodies of the actors mass together forming a gigantic silhouette, a groaning organic being, monstrous but nobly conceived: the creation of Frankenstein.

The Jailbreak is inspired by Frankenstein. It ends with a fire in which all of the prisoners are killed: the rebellion has failed because it was rooted in violence. The smoke clears and the prisoners lie dead. Silence. The structure is silhouetted again, and a countdown begins as the actors once again form the Creature; this time he is literally the mass, the dramatic representation of mankind. He looms above the stage and drops a net. On the count of zero he sweeps the audience with a searchlight: the tools of oppression are not so easily discarded. A second's pause, and the implements are laid aside; the arms open upward in peace and love: the tree of life. The alternative has been found. Zero has been passed. Can man be raised this time?

But Are They Really Actors?

For God's sake, who wants actors?

Je veux avec l'hiéroglyphe d'un souffle retrouver une idée du théâtre sacré. ARTAUD

The most recurrent questions about the Living Theatre concern its dramatic technique. Do they practice yoga? What kind of formal training do they go through? In answer to the first question, "In a way," and a perhaps embarrassing "None" to the second, and yet the achievements on stage and in the theatre are often fantastic. Certain points must be clarified immediately:

First, because it is a constantly moving, completely nomadic community, the Living Theatre cannot hold formal rehearsals and workshops. Country to country, city to city, its "homes" are hotel rooms where there is no space to rehearse, if time could be found to begin with. On the other hand, they perform on the average of two hundred nights a year;[1] they are trained by the necessity of performing.

Another important factor evolves from their anarchistic

---

[1]During the 203 days in the United States, there were 126 performances in theatres, two television shows, plus several paid lecture-demonstrations and a few free or benefit performances.

73

ideals; anyone can be an actor, a performer. "Acting is not making believe, but living exquisitely in the moment": Henry Howard. The Living Theatre isn't concerned with dramatic technique; the technique they are concerned with is *magic,* they look for miracles. Their exploration is, in the words of Cocteau, of "a zone of man to which man can not descend, even if Virgil were to lead him . . . for Virgil would not go down here."[2] From this abysmal horror comes the birth of creation; in the twofold voyage from life to death and from death to a new life, nonbeing is reborn into being. The trip is the experience, an exorcism of personal demons which at the same time will be therapeutically beneficial. As the psychotic experience goes beyond the rationale of common sense, so the "technique" of the Living Theatre may more rightfully belong to the realm of psychiatry than to that of theatrical preparation.

Au théâtre poésie et science doivent désormais s'identifier. ANTONIN ARTAUD

The following from Ronald Laing[3] defines the role of the actor and the function of the play:

Among physicians and priests there should be some who are guides, who can educt the person from this world and educt him to the other. To guide him in it; and to lead him back again. (the actor)

One enters the other world by breaking a shell: or through a door: through a partition: the curtains part or rise: a veil is lifted. Seven veils: seven seals, seven heavens. (the play)

[2]R. D. Laing, *The Politics of Experience* (London: Penguin Books), 1967.
[3]*Ibid.*

Three groups of philosophical influences are closely inter-related in the Living Theatre's basic technique: yoga and tantric doctrines; the concepts of Artaud; and, both ideally and practically, the anarchistic-communitarian beliefs. Awareness of the constant threat of destruction leads to the only possible alternative: creation. Civilization destroys feeling and the organic process of emotion. Behavior is formalized; we are programmed to suffocate the genuine self. Little contact remains between the artistic creation and life; they have drifted apart when life should be the only form of art. In his exalted state of perception, the artist, as the human being with a vestigial sensory antenna still remaining, must realize and assume his responsibility to the life process. In the emergency referred to by Laing as "the dreadful already happened," it remains for the artist to give hope, to answer with creation.

But more important than any of its philosophical influences, the art (craftsmanship) of the Living Theatre is the direct product of its years together, living communally, traveling, suffering, getting busted, getting high, raving, loving, freaking out, being hungry, being poor, being loved and hated, but always being together in that dreadful already happened. Almost a culture in itself, the Living is a community of strongly individual people who have learned, through a tenuously balanced fortune of misery and acclaim, to live together, not necessarily because they all love one another, but primarily because they cannot live with anyone else, they cannot function within a conventional community. The result is a magical understanding in a unique *here and now,* a form of communication that approaches the metaphysical. In relating to the group, the individual's energy and experience are taken and transformed into a communal energy and experience; it is a constant process of feedback and recharge.

"The ground of the being of all beings is the relationship between them." R.D. LAING. It is in performances where the truest relationship is established, where One-ness is created out of each individual's awareness of the others' "vocabulary" in terms of limitations and dynamics.

The term "yoga" denotes only the derivation of the physical and psychic exercises employed to uncover the spiritual essence of man, his supreme being. Yoga is not an end in itself, but a technical means of achieving that result. Similarities occur between Tantric doctrine . . . and modern physics. Are the atoms of our bodies different from those that form galaxies? Man is the microcosm of a macrocosm. Every man is a universe and part of the same universe, possessing in his being the same divine power of the universe. "He who realizes the bodily truth will know the truth of the universe." *Prâna* denotes both the universal vital energy and the process of breathing. The breathing itself is a nonspoken prayer (*Ajapa Mantra*). On the physical level this *prâna* is manifested in the human body as inhaling and exhaling. This is the same rhythm as the creative cosmic process . . . we are all part of the same organism. It is the movement of the return to the source; the opposite of the creative movement originated by the source.

In the Tantric *maithuna* (ritual sexual union) we not only have the destruction of the individual ego in order to attain the state of supreme selflessness, but also the union

76

of opposites, the fusion of two different polarities through which flows the cosmic energy.

Intellectual knowledge of such mystical doctrines is of less import than the direct experience derived from their practical application. Concerning breathing, for example, absolute concentration (or meditation) begins with a proper breathing pattern, with simply learning *how to breathe*. By slowing or accelerating the breathing rhythm, different levels of energy are created, and both physical and mental changes occur; it is possible to obtain control of certain organic functions—blood circulation, fear, anger, hunger, etc. Sound is a manifestation of a certain vibratory energy. Different parts of our systems react to different sound vibrations. In the theatre, different moods can be created by effecting a chemical change in the bodies of the audience.

"Teach us, Lama, the material levitation of bodies and how we might no longer be held by the earth!" was the anguished cry of Antonin Artaud. "Nous sommes bien décidés à faire une Révolution": Artaud's *Declaration du 27 Janvier 1925*. By 1933 *the street* was for him the only place in which theatre might have any genuine meaning for the people. Like the closing of the circle, all is one: magic is the esthetic for the revolution; community is necessary for the full self-realization of the individual, for the surrealistic explosion that leads to anarchy and to freedom. We must, *with* and *inside* of our beings, discover the "physical, objective element understandable to everyone." We must break down the barriers to get to the few feelings still alive; we must re-form the magic chain. Burning with cruelty,

77

meaning the rigour, the implacable and irreversible dedication, the hallucination and the lucid consciousness, the painful joy of creation. To understand the work of the Living Theatre it is necessary to understand Artaud, to know that his concepts form the spine of that work.

"Before evaluating culture, I must consider that the world is hungry; and that it is not concerned with culture; and that it is through deception that we wish to orient toward culture thoughts that are directed only toward hunger."[4]

---

[4]*Le Théâtre et Son Double,* Antonin Artaud; Gallimard; or, *The Theatre and Its Double*; Grove Press: a terribly lifeless translation compared to the brilliant style of the original work.

Organization of the Tour

Several individuals had lent financial assistance (and the New York State Council of the Arts had given a $4,500 grant) to bring the Living Theatre back, but there were three people directly involved with the organization and production of the tour. This is not a particularly heartening side of the story, for it was a shame that the Living Theatre could not (or did not bother to) find a more capable staff to represent and manage its business interest. Of these three producers, only Beverly Landau would appear to possess sufficient background and professional ability, but she relinquished an active participation fairly early in the course of events, leaving the field open for a sort of running gun battle between Mel Howard and Saul Gottlieb, the other producers.

No matter what truth or what lies are buried in the endless flow of accusations and rebuttals, no matter what the basis (if any) or the eventual outcome (if any) of threatened lawsuits and investigations, the impression is that they all (including the company, which allowed it to happen) deserved one another, either because they were too stupid to realize the importance of what was at stake, or too avaricious to care. The initial fault lies with the Becks' having accepted such a situation for their company, and if it could later be observed that the Living Theatre's tour had been produced by "artistically pretentious slum landlords," sympathy was short because it was an almost intentional bid for victimization on the part of the Becks, and such self-defeating maneuvres soon become tiresome. It must be said, just to balance the scales, that it's doubtful if any producer, or group of producers, no matter how competent, experienced or well intentioned they might be, could have handled this venture without difficulty. The setup of the company itself and its tendency to regard all businessmen, and therefore all producers, as crooks suggests only part of the problem, while the face to face business attitude of the Becks is, at best, one of condescension. Even supposedly non-businessmen types . . . film-makers, writers, photographers . . . are put through uncalled for numbers . . . evasions, delaying tactics, word games and ridiculously petty criticism . . . when what is being requested may ultimately be useful or favorable to the company. However, in this particular case, two of the producers were conspicuously ill-equipped for the enterprise and the third was simply misguided in her good intentions.

In his early thirties, Mel Howard lived for several years in Paris where he had produced thirty-some plays and had owned a cabaret on the Left Bank. While maintaining certain theatrical interests abroad, he returned to the States about five years ago and began importing European theatre groups for college and university tours. For the most part, choice of productions was on a decidedly academic level, being neither distinctive nor adventurous, suggesting rather a dubious nostalgia for the *kitsch* of the Fifties. Despite this presumably dedicated theatrical involvement, while living abroad and on subsequent return trips, he saw the Living Theatre for the first time on opening night in New Haven, because, as he put it, he might as well see what he was selling and find out what all the fuss was about.

Beverly Landau had produced and co-produced many notable plays, both on- and Off-Broadway. Her connection with the Living Theatre dated back to before their European departure when she had been among those who were trying to raise money to reopen *The Brig* in New York and to finance its subsequent London production. The outcome of these earlier efforts had been Julian Beck's decision not to accept "outside investment" for the reopening of *The Brig* in New York, and the investors who had thus been cut out of the New York production were no longer interested in the London engagement, which was then taken over by English entrepreneur Oscar Lewenstein. This phase ended in September of 1964 when *The Brig* was presented at London's Mermaid Theatre.

About a year and a half ago Beverly was contacted by a friend, New York photographer and artist Carl Bissenger, also a long-time friend of the Becks, who ever since their departure had been among the many concerned with bringing them back. Interest was reawakened, but this time it was frustrated with the discovery that producer-director Leo Garen held the production rights to the Living Theatre's return. Garen had paid no money for these rights; nevertheless, he owned the option, a factor that tied up the possibility of anyone else bringing the Living Theatre over until its expiration. End of this phase.

81

While waiting for the Garen rights to expire and the introduction of the third party involved in the operation of the current tour, a brief digression: As it was to turn out, Beverly Landau chose to play a less active role—aside from the investment of over $7,000 of her own money—in the numerous unnecessary and completely avoidable complications that set in almost immediately at the business end of this tour. As the only woman connected with it, her choice is understandable, but, more importantly, as someone with a distinctly professional approach to work, it is more likely that she withdrew out of discouragement, leaving the other two to hang in and fight it out.

The third party was Saul Gottlieb, a writer and poet whose connection with the Living Theatre goes back to his performances in some of their early productions. Gottlieb was also active as a producer and director in the early Off-Broadway movement; however, the reputation that has survived the longest is one of political activism, despite its being rooted in the oldest Left of the thirties and forties. Gottlieb's involvement is explicable only in terms of the Radical Theatre Repertory, which, with him as its official representative,[1] ostensibly functioned as a sponsoring organization for the Living Theatre's tour. The Radical Theatre Repertory came into theoretical existence about two years ago. The beginnings of its practical functions prior to the Living Theatre tour are

[1]Richard Schechner, editor of the *Tulane Drama Review* at that time and director of the Performance Group, is president of the Radical Theatre Repertory; Saul Gottlieb holds the title of treasurer. Schechner, unhappy with the way it was being handled, resigned as nominal president of RTR when the Living Theatre tour was barely underway.

rather nebulous, but it is known at least one theatrical benefit was held to support it. It was originally conceived as a booking agency for the collective of Off-Broadway and experimental theatre groups—La Mama, the Open Theatre, the Bread and Puppet Theatre, the Pageant Players, the Theatre of the Ridiculous, and the Performance Group being the most notable of such ensembles to have participated in the vagaries of the Repertory in the past couple of years. Almost by definition RTR was loosely organized, non-profit, and prone to much in-fighting among the directors of its member groups whenever tighter organization was attempted. Since much time was lost by individual directors in the booking and business end of their operations, there seemed to be no question that the idea of such a collective was a good one. And it is also possible that, had it been properly set up and managed, further benefits could have been derived through foundation grants to the Repertory as a whole. However, inasmuch as one of the groups tentatively aligned had already received individual grants from various sources, their directors weren't overly enthusiastic about financial aid that would have to be apportioned among all of the member groups. Despite its conceptual advantages, the Radical Theatre Repertory had foundered, the primary reason being that it lacked competent and capable leadership to conduct its business. It had remained a good idea and was not really activated or incorporated until March of 1968 when the Living Theatre tour was in the wind.

Through Carl Bissinger and a few others with the same interest in the Living Theatre, Saul Gottlieb heard of Beverly

83

Landau and contacted her. By this time, April of 1968, Leo Garen's option had expired and Gottlieb had since maintained steady contact with the Becks, whose interest in a return tour appeared to be quite concrete. The main concern of these potential producers and investors was To Bring the Living Theatre Back. Now was the time, politically and artistically; it was important to bring them back; the American theatre needed them; and so forth. Besides, the Becks-Gottlieb correspondence indicated that they wanted to come, and there seemed to be enough people willing to get involved to keep business under control.

From the very beginning of this project, money was a major problem. There were two important European debts owed by the company, and one of them had to be settled before it left for the States; the other investor was willing to wait and be repaid from the early returns on American engagements, but the terms of both reimbursements would have to be arranged out front. On top of this, Julian, wiser after the Garen affair, was now insisting upon a $3,000 option in the event that nothing came of the present negotiations; $1,000 apiece was put up between Landau, Gottlieb and a friend of his, Bruce Grund. At this point, Ellen Stewart, director of the La Mama troupe, set up a meeting between Beverly Landau and Michael Butler, producer of *Hair*, who wanted to produce the Living Theatre on Broadway. The Becks rejected this from Europe, and from the Old Left, Gottlieb put Butler down as a "capitalist." Later on, however, after a large portion of the tour had been set up Butler agreed to guarantee $10,000 with his travel agent for the return fares with the understanding that the sponsoring organization, the Radical Theatre Repertory, would be responsible for the payment of this sum over a limited period of time. In other words, Butler invested no money, but acted in the capacity of a business reference who was guaranteeing the specified amount to the travel agent in order to ensure the company's return travel tickets. When the date of expiration arrived only $4,000 of the $10,000 had been paid by Gottlieb, and Butler withdrew his guarantee.

But Butler's initial interest in the Living Theatre having been turned down by the Becks, Beverly Landau then went to Mel Howard, who agreed to meet Saul Gottlieb to talk about the project. It was summer by this time and the money talk still sounded hopeless, though everyone was still agreeing that Yes, It Would Be Nice To Bring The Living Theatre Back. From the outset of this first meeting it seemed obvious that Gottlieb's estimate of the initial investment needed could use at least one more zero behind it. Besides the previously mentioned option rights and loans from investors abroad, something would certainly have to be done (aside from the producers paying them) about the 1959-1963 tax debt that was still owed the federal government; this would entail the hiring of legal representatives and accountants before the company even arrived, because, theoretically at least, the Becks could be arrested on disembarkation. And then there were "about thirty," according to Gottlieb, members of the company and nine children, all of whom would have to be brought over and supported for the duration of the tour. Just getting the Living Theatre to the Atlantic Ocean, not even across it, would be a revolutionary act in itself. It sounded hopeless and slightly crazy, too, but still

85

It Would Be Nice-and-so-forth, and somewhere in the course of this meeting, Mel Howard agreed to book the Living Theatre's tour, because it was easier, he said, than explaining how to do it to the head of the Radical Theatre Repertory.

Under Saul Gottlieb's self-election as its treasurer and guiding force, the Radical Theatre Repertory is whipped into a state of corporate entity, which will partially explain its role as sponsor of the Living Theatre's tour. It is understood between the company (the Becks) and the major parties involved at this end that as a precaution against possible reprisals by the federal government in connection with the unpaid back taxes, nothing is to be in the name of the Living Theatre. It is suggested that a special corporation be formed. Gottlieb argues that the RTR is now incorporated; it can handle the Living Theatre—another corporation isn't necessary. Landau and Howard are opposed to this, since one of the things they have agreed upon is that under a separate corporation Howard will book the tour, and investment money and profits will be under legal supervision, and the Living Theatre will produce itself; it is assumed Julian understood this, inasmuch as he has been informed of the feasibility and advantages of this arrangement. This, of course, will limit Gottlieb's direct involvement by eliminating any need for his Repertory, and he is determined not to let this happen. By dragging things on and wasting time (it is now past the mid-summer mark), he finally succeeds in making it "easier" for the others to give in and let RTR take the Living Theatre under its aegis. In

86

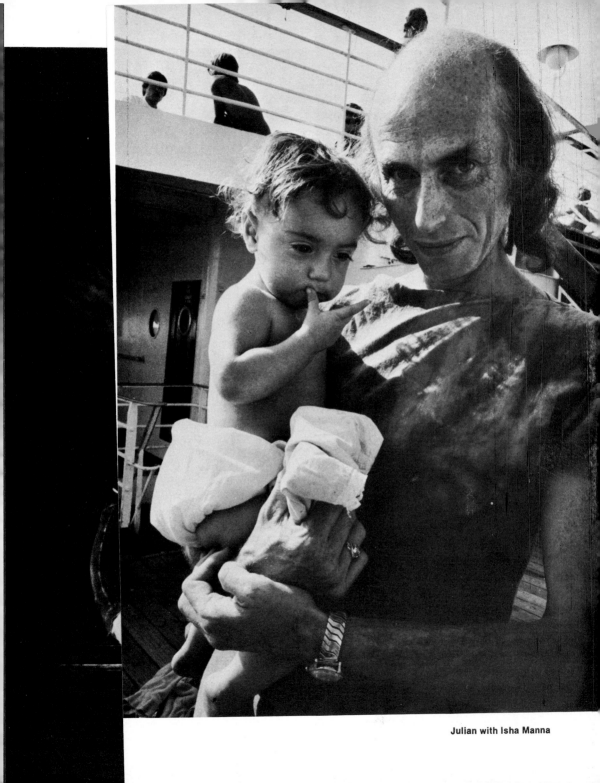

Julian with Isha Manna

Act III. The prison

The Creature / end of Act III

New Haven courtroom after the bust

The company chanting with Allen Ginsberg /
dressing room, Brooklyn Academy of Music

Creon's guards come to imprison Antigone (Judith Malina, *foreground*); *in background*, the Dance of Bacchus has begun

Antigone *(background)* mourns as the Thebans celebrate their false victory over Argos

The blind seer Tiresias (Rufus Collins) comes to warn the Thebans. This photograph was taken at Avignon during the Theatre Festival of 1968. Seated in the background, their mouths sealed with tape, another company of actors who have been invited onstage to protest the closing by local authorities of their political play

The Becks as Antigone and Creon

view of everything else, this is a minor point in the arguments by now. Besides, Julian has been persuaded to go along with this "old friend of the Living Theatre," rather than with these strangers whose commercial interests may not be aligned with those of his company.

And that issue having been settled, the RTR has an official function, which means that the directors of its member ensembles are invited to participate in endless meetings with the Gottlieb-Howard-Landau contingent and argue into the night about the impending tour. Starting on a level of aesthetic principles and Yes, It Would Be Nice, etc., things accelerate, and the meetings take on a peculiar savagery that only radicals can achieve when the subject at hand is "a piece of the action." But before that point is reached, Ellen Stewart withdraws La Mama's further participation in the Repertory, bestows a decidedly sacrilegious blessing on its future and that of its officers, and leaves in disgust. The meetings continue, until an agreement is eventually reached and contracts are drawn up between Mel Howard and Beverly Landau and Saul Gottlieb as representative of the RTR. The next step is the negotiation of a contract between these three and the Becks, and Gottlieb flies to Avignon to work on that.

Normally this isn't a particularly complicated thing to handle, but in this case, when it got beyond the standard contractual agreements the impression on this side of the Atlantic was that maybe the Living Theatre didn't really want to come after all. Almost daily Gottlieb's transatlantic calls relayed some unexpected "emergency," some new demand that would have to be either met or countered—they would not travel at all by plane; many members, including the Becks, were afraid to fly. Instead a large caravan of small buses was requested, each of which would transport six people and their luggage. It was pointed out that this arrangement would permit more mobility for those in the company who might wish to travel beyond the appointed destinations. Having themselves spent time with other productions in some of the appointed destinations, the producers instantly rejected this plan; mobility would not guarantee performances between New York and the Coast. A compromise was reached that did agree to the bussing stipulation, but the amount of time and energy wasted and performances lost because of this transportation would be incalculable in the end.

Some rejected demands: they asked for a guarantee that baby-sitters would be hired and paid for by the producers; they wanted to bring over the Volkswagen buses owned by the company in Europe, with a guarantee that the producers would be responsible for the sale of these vehicles in America at the end of the tour, the money from the sales being sent to them in Europe. Placed in the unaccepted position of used car dealers and employers of baby-sitters, the producers were then instructed as to how many days off were required each week by the company, and limitations were placed on the number of miles to be covered in a day's travel between bookings.

It was a dance. How much of it was based on a desire to give the Americans a hard time and how much was motivated by negative expectations is a matter of speculation. Considering the troubles and hardships experienced during the European years, the latter is a perfectly reasonable attitude, and it would hardly make sense for them to come back to America to face the same conditions. Yet it is known that in Avignon, Julian had warned the company that the return trip could be disastrous; he had anticipated serious trouble and his attitude had not been encouraging. Why then had he already agreed to come?

They had to. Despite their popularity and large following among the artists and intellectuals of Europe, they did have a limited repertory,[2] and no matter how highly acclaimed this repertory remained, the Living Theatre was rapidly using up its audience, and *Paradise Now* had only made it more limited: it had been well received by public officials and the conservative majority at the Festival of Avignon, but riots had broken out after its premiere; nor had Geneva taken kindly to the public demonstrations following performances there (on arriving in New York, the company learned that future performances of *Paradise Now* had been banned in Geneva). In other words, they needed new exposure, and the offer of an American tour was perfectly timed. As for America, there were those who remembered their work and its vast contributions to breaking down theatrical conventions here, particularly *here* in New York, for they had had little recognition beyond New York before now. Almost the entire country could be reached now, but most important was the generation of young people who had never heard of the Living Theatre; here was a new audience. American publicity would be advantageous on the return to Europe—for a while, anyway. It was a gamble, a terrible one, really, but win or lose, it had to be done.

[2]Besides the four productions, all performed for the first time in the United States on this tour, the European repertory included *The Brig* and *The Maids*.

89

The Tour Begins: Discovery of America

It is necessary to give some information on the logistics of the Living. After the New Haven and Brooklyn engagements, both attended by what is called "a New York audience," the discovery of America really began. Plane and train transportation having been refused by the company, an attempt was made to arrange the bookings with an eye toward logistic convenience, an admirable effort that often failed because of the success of the publicity from the New Haven-New York runs. Geographic convenience then became the deciding factor, and from mid-October through the Christmas holidays we remained in the Northeast; Vermont to Philadelphia, Stony Brook to Detroit the directional encompassments. It wasn't until January that the long westward trek began from Chicago; it had reached California by mid-February, and finally the eastbound return set out from San Francisco on the eleventh of March. There were no bookings on the return leg. The destination was Boston for a third run, this one two performances at the Ark Theatre, and then back to the Brooklyn Academy of Music for the final engagement before going back to Europe in early April . . . .

But back to mid-October and the end of the "New York audiences." The following caravan of rented wheeled vehicles has been provided to transport (transmit) the company coast to coast: the Big Bus, driven by Tony Hawley, carries most of the entourage and luggage and is equipped with the usual basic Big Bus necessities, including a toilet (its interior is soon personalized with various decorative effects, the most standard of these being red and purple gels over the seat lights); a small white bus that carries eight people who have usually come close to renouncing nonviolence in order to escape the Big Bus when, on a moment's notice, the BB is transformed into a mobile mental ward; an eight-passenger red bus, the Beckmobile, carrying Judith and Julian, Isha, Pierre Biner, and three or four others; an ancient green schoolbus, purchased by Bill and Dorothy Shari to carry themselves and three of their children—this schoolbus, mechanical temperament overshadowing its charm, was one of those baroque luxuries that you usually buy when you have something else; a red Volkswagen driven by Gianfranco and myself, its four-seater capacity converted into that of an ostentatious shopping cart in order to accommodate luggage, typewriter, cameras and tape recorder and, on the way back from California, a four-foot cactus that attracted aesthetic approval in the Arizona desert; and finally, frequently victimized by snowstorms, the *Frankenstein* truck.

The official entourage consists of thirty-four Living: at the start, nine children ranging in age from a little more than a year to seven years, by the end, thirteen children, the eldest being around fourteen; road managers Bob Cohen and Mark

Amitin; Pierre Biner, Swiss journalist and author of *Le Living Théâtre*, who is following the tour and who has been assigned the duties of company archivist and secretary to Julian; Moon Nimon, moon maiden on terrestrial voyage, she is Isha's baby-sitter; Susan Sutton, pretty and English, her trip begins in Boston where she has been hired to sell the Living Theatre poetry books at performances; Tony Hawley, commander of the Big Bus; and myself, whose function is often open to debate. At certain points en route the following changes and confusions occur:

In Portland, Oregon, Bob Cohen is replaced by Mark Amitin as road manager; in Ashland, Oregon, the next stop, this appears not to be the case. The company now has two road managers, a prestigious development diminished only by the simultaneous development that the company cannot be paid that week. Berkeley, the next stop: Cohen sends his resignation to the Radical Theatre Repertory; L. A., RTR fires Amitin (who hasn't been paid for several weeks) when he calls Gottlieb to find out if Cohen's resignation has arrived yet. On advice of legal counsel, Amitin must return to New York as soon as possible; he borrows more money from relatives and gets on an airplane, thus becoming the first evidence in six months that man can fly. San Francisco, last stop: Cohen is once again "hired," but it doesn't matter. No one's getting paid anyway. Reasons to be gone into later.

Moon Nimon meets an old boyfriend in Boston and resigns from her position as baby-sitter; she later pops up in L. A. where she and boyfriend have ended their cross-country migration, and where she does *not* rejoin the en-

93

tourage, a singular distinction in itself. Her baby-sitting replacement is Susan Sutton. Mel Clay is joined by his wife and three-year-old son, Gino; Jim Anderson is joined by his son, Niles, aged four. By California practically everyone has been joined and the grand total of officials and joiners is more than sixty men, women, and children. This figure is exclusive of the hangers-on and hangers-in whose totals change at every stop and whose mysterious means of locomotion seem fueled only by an unswerving dedication to hanging-in. The quantity and quality of this accumulation, many of them permanent fixtures from coast to coast, generally serve to illustrate the principles of inertia and indicate that the perfect vacuum is not far off.

From the outset the tour showed every evidence of being a financial success for the Living Theatre and there was no tenable reason for it not to have been. On paper it had been well plotted beforehand and many bookings had to be turned down. Between private investments and advance ticket sales, the first months looked solvent and it could even be anticipated that by the end the Living Theatre would go back to Europe with a good-size profit. But the terrible fact is that, due to the mismanagement and ineptitude of the Radical Theatre Repertory, the profit feedback worked in inverse proportion to the company's cross-country progression. Practically everywhere it performed the Living Theatre played to capacity audiences, and whether the reaction of the public and local critics was good or bad, auditoriums, theatres, and gymnasiums were filled as the public came out to see what all the fuss was about. There were exceptions, the most significant being in Berkeley and San Francisco, but these

94

were unusual and most often due to specific conditions existing within the given communities. To cite examples, the RTR-arranged three-day booking in Kansas City, Kansas happened to coincide with mid-term vacations for the colleges in the area. However, the one performance there of *Paradise Now* drew a larger crowd than the total of the previous performances of *Mysteries* and *Antigone,* and the Living were received like a polymorphous Messiah after bringing Paradise to Kansas City. The Detroit Institute of Art, where two years before a concert by the Budapest String Quartet was picketed by right-wing elements, was nervous about pushing the Living Theatre's advance ticket sales too far, and there were one or two other places where sales just crossed the break-even mark.

Moneywise, *Paradise* brought in most of it, primarily through the enormous student-audiences attracted to it. Since it was also capable of attracting trouble as well, its performances were generally scheduled on the closing night (or nights, if it got past the first one) of a run. There was also another good reason for this; if it was presented first, or early, in a run, the other plays risked disruption by students who felt it their privilege to take part in all the plays. *Frankenstein* was the second most successful, first on programs where *Paradise* wasn't included. From the point of view of both the public and the critics it was by far the favorite, and there were only one or two occasions when it wasn't completely sold out. *Antigone* was next, and here I believe it was simply a matter of the American public being put off by the idea of paying money to see what they expected to be a classic performed by a reputedly avant-

95

garde theatre ensemble. It is doubtful that any theatre group, avant or derriere, could have changed this preconception very much, since the local critics in many areas passed over its relevance in favor of regionally imbedded opinion that was generally shallow. Ironically, it was better received by students, possibly because they had a closer familiarity with the Sophocles play and wanted to see what the Living Theatre did with it.

Oddly enough, in view of its tremendous welcome opening night at Yale, *Mysteries* proved to be a consistent loser except when it was presented on one- or two-night stands. It was usually reserved as the matinee attraction when matinees were scheduled, which was very seldom, two shows a day being much too fatiguing for the company. As a single-performance booking *Mysteries* worked well, and there were many occasions when audiences were so completely shaken up by The Plague that they solemnly assisted in carrying the "dead" bodies back to the body pile; they often cried out and invoked God's mercy, and at the performance at Brown University in Providence, to cite but one example, students came onstage and administered first aid and mouth-to-mouth breathing to "the dying." There were times when they reacted with college humor and wise-ass interference with the cast, particularly with Gene Gordon in the beginning, but the incense ritual and "The Chord" were usually reliable calmatives. But then there was a particularly unsettling experience at Denison University, in an apparently reactionary Ohio community, where a one-night engagement elicited near-violence and a frighteningly fascistic response from students triggered by the antiwar, nonviolent

96

slogans of the "Street Songs." But more surprising than this was that it was *Mysteries,* tame and conventional in comparison to any of the other plays, that had aroused them to this rage; they hadn't even seen *Paradise.* After the Denison engagement (where during The Plague students had tried to carry "the dead" out of the gymnasium and load the bodies into cars) precautions were taken whenever an audience appeared to be even mildly aggressive; bodyguards were discreetly posted in the rear of the aisles to prevent physical attacks on the actors.

Paradise Now drew an entirely different audience from those who attended the other plays. *Frankenstein* and *Antigone* attracted the more serious theatre-going public, even in campus theatres where there was often an equal proportion of student and older, non-student spectators; *Mysteries* drew a mixed bag, the students responding more favorably than the older spectators, who seldom responded in any appreciable manner until the wipe-out of The Plague. But *Paradise Now* was invariably a freak show, a predictably chaotic event that rarely achieved the aesthetic and spiritual aspirations its collective creators had set for it. Although many of its spectator-participants, especially the young ones, were alleged to have been changed or at least very turned-on by it, from personal observation, having gone through more of *Paradise* than is necessary to relate, I believe that a majority of these people could have been changed or turned-on by anything, and there appeared to be a grave necessity for clearing up a semantic confusion: *There is a difference between "hippies" and people who are hip.* Which of us clings to the better delusion will ultimately

97

depend not upon which of us changes the world first, but which of us can survive it now with a minimum of brain damage.

Between the hippies and the hip there are the squares, presumably those who in one way or another are older, those who in their psychic rigidity cannot be blown apart, and their reaction to *Paradise* was as boringly predictable as that of the hippies. It would have been a social phenomenon to have found anyone over twenty-one in an audience by the end of *Paradise*. A mild exaggeration, but an unfortunate prevailing condition, because it was this older, rigid segment of the spectator public that should have been reached, that should have been encouraged to express themselves. More than anyone else, they need this catharsis. They were the ones who might have grasped the more profound intentions of *Paradise,* who might have been forced to come to grips with a reality that isn't only within the domain of the youthful conscience. Inhibited and constricted as it was, a more serious effort should have been exerted to reach this square audience; to turn them on would have been a greater challenge, for even a tiny alteration in their thinking would amount to a triumph. This may be overrating the talent and ability of the Living Theatre—it may even sound square —but given their energy and avowed dedication (delusion?) to change the world, it doesn't seem like a terribly grotesque notion. But with the square (and all too frequently this applied to anyone whose rebuttal couldn't be converted into support) open to verbal assault and laceration that might callous a hardened psyche or atrophy an already crippled ego, the arena was left for the hippie who had come to freak out, to skim off the superficial trappings that appealed to him, to worship the intellectual pretentiousness that smoke-screened the artistic merits of *Paradise*. As a result, *Paradise Now* became the magnetic force that drew a horde of loose human particles across the country, and because of the over-blown and usually misleading publicity from two busts (New Haven and Philadelphia) and a ban (Cambridge), it would be the cause of all anxiety among deans, trustees, and local police and fire marshals. And as far ahead as Los Angeles a dean would still be waiting to prevent them from bringing *Paradise* to the University of Southern California.

October 31–November 8: Massachusetts Institute of Technology, Cambridge, Mass.

Since everyday is Halloween with the Living, the official one was notable only for the opening of *Frankenstein* at MIT's Kresge Auditorium. Much enthusiasm greeted the opening, and all performances for the ten-day run were sold out. Along with the first prophetic wave of followers and groupies, we had also acquired a media contingent of film-makers, television documentarians, and magazine and press people. But only part of the attention was concentrated on the Living Theatre.

Michael O'Connor, an AWOL soldier, was staying at the student center at MIT, where he had requested, and had been granted, sanctuary in his protest against the Vietnam war. Because of the nature of his alleged crime, only FBI agents could come onto the premises to arrest him, and there was a constant flux of resistance activity in the student center—posters, leaflets, speeches, petitions, sit-ins, and milling crowds of students and professors at all hours of the day and late into the night. Waiting, waiting. It was expected, perhaps even hoped—for only then would resolution come—that the Feds would come on the weekend. Amidst a science-fiction landscape of futuristic architecture where everyone appeared asexual and plugged into all manner of unimaginable space age wizardry—heavy test-tube activity, space freaks, and Laser weirdos—it was difficult to believe that an institution dedicated to and totally dependent upon technological research would be concerned with peace, yet there was a strong resistance movement on campus.

After the opening performance, the Living was invited to the Sanctuary. Dick Gregory had been scheduled to appear, but he had been forced to cancel because of illness; the film that was also scheduled hadn't arrived. Would the Living please come over and do something? They had accepted and had appeared with the plan to bring everyone together with a "Chord." But the students wanted more direct action, a demonstration—*do* something! On the grounds that the methods suggested would only lead to a violent confrontation with local authorities, the Living had declined. Then what should we do? the students asked.

"Get the fuck out of MIT," advised a spokesman for the company, and the Living left.

The company reportedly felt that here was another instance of students hoping to use them to trigger a violent situation; the Sanctuary, actively comprised of students and members of the faculty, felt that the company had let them down by refusing to support their protest action, which was significant in that this was the first strongly endorsed resistance action at MIT and it had consolidated large numbers of students, faculty, and Cambridge residents in support of O'Connor. If the Living's reasons for not participating were valid, those of the Sanctuary were equally so; possibly more so, inasmuch as the Living's support had been sought and had, in the opinion of many, been dismissed too easily; getting the fuck out of MIT doesn't solve the problem, it just makes room for those anxious to get into it. A split developed in which the Sanctuary's opinion of the Living was summed up by one of its faculty supporters: "They're just a bunch of bullshit actors and hippies." In turn, the Sanctuary didn't lend their support to the Living Theatre when the MIT administration canceled performances after the first *Paradise Now*.

Tuesday, November 5: Election Day

The first *Paradise*, the straight Bostonians have fled, the theatre is jammed with serious young dissidents and the spaced-out curious. In the dressing room downstairs a transistor radio broadcasts the early election returns, and Judith sits making scrupulous notations on a chart, a scorecard for inertia . . . Humphrey, Nixon, Wallace, Eldridge Cleaver, only the latter connected with the True State of the Union, and because of that, having the least hopes of being elected. Just beginning to come in, the returns are slow and repetitious, indifference being the feedback from the characters of

101

the two forerunning contenders. Upstairs in the auditorium the audience is in upheaval, screaming and shouting, and being shouted down for being . . . indifferent. I leave to check out the Sanctuary. . . .

Empty. Except for a handful of students clustered near the entrance, whispering, then furtively dispersing when the door is opened. A young girl stops a second and then approaches. "You're with the Living Theatre," she doesn't ask, "Go and tell them to get rid of their drugs immediately . . . Michael O'Connor is in the theatre, and the Feds are here to bust him and the Living Theatre, if they can."

The auditorium lobby is full of plainclothesmen and one of them stops me. No one is allowed in or out . . . anymore. I insist that I'm "Press," my things are in the dressing room and I must get them back. He answers: "We know what's down there." Outside the building, more of them, and I sneak in through an unattended delivery entrance. Word spreads quickly among the actors onstage and discreet exits are made for the dressing room. Minutes later Cathy, rearranged into a "straight" appearance, leaves the campus with a tattered shopping bag. The dressing room has been cleaned.

And suddenly the election returns are interrupted by a BULLETIN! . . . *the Cambridge police are raiding the Kresge Auditorium where the Living Theatre is performing* Paradise Now! *They are arresting the performers and war resistor Michael O'Connor.* . . .

It's hard to describe what goes through your mind when an authoritative voice bulletins in that you're in the process of being arrested, when in reality you're sitting with a few

102

people in loincloths listening to the radio, but for a split-second it's so abstract that you're "Staying Tuned For Further Details." Maybe it's happening upstairs in the theatre. . . .

And that's even more confusing, because the fuzz have vacated the lobby; the theatre doors, closed and guarded but minutes ago, are now wide open. If anything, the bedlam of the show has accelerated, and misdemeanors, assaults and batteries, and extreme mental cruelty can be witnessed all the way back to the dressing room. . . .

. . . Where someone is suggesting that the bulletin is a warning to the company that something *may* happen—a curious notion because when an actual alert was given by someone aware of the situation as it was going down in the lobby and outside the theatre, this same party obliquely dismissed it as some terribly meddlesome expression of paranoia. That the inexplicated radio bulletin can be interpreted as a conspiratorial harbinger is by no means an altogether improbable idea. But as paranoia goes, that's not bad either.

It is later learned that Michael O'Connor, apparently giving more credence to his own warning system, left the theatre when the police arrived. A small group from the Sanctuary stand in the lobby. A professor among them vociferously expresses the feelings they share with the young soldier and the purity of his protest, and the Living Theatre is indicted in what appears to be a case of negligence caused by irresponsibility due to lack of awareness. Do they think that nudity in this theatre is new? Do they believe that chaos in there to be a solution for anything? Do they even

103

think it's interesting? No one argues with the professor; what argument can there be? The subject returns to Michael O'Connor.

O'Connor left because there were too many obvious excuses for a raid on the theatre. Smoking in the auditorium, possession of marijuana and other drugs, nudity: any or all of these were readily in evidence among the spectators. A raid would not only put an end to the disorderly performance and get rid of its most likely instigator, the Living Theatre, it would also net O'Connor and put an end to the Sanctuary movement. Which of these had police priority could be ascertained by the curtailment of the raid on finding that the AWOL soldier had left the building. For O'Connor to be arrested under the given circumstances would be unworthy of his cause: drugs and nudity would be played up by the press as a smokescreen to cheapen and distort his serious protest of the war. O'Connor was said to have been forced to enlist in the army to avoid a prison sentence for possession of marijuana. The issue of his resistance could easily have been clouded had the raid taken place. He was taken into custody and court-martialed without fanfare after the Living Theatre had left.

On the night following *Paradise* at MIT there was a single performance of *Mysteries* at Brown University, after which we were supposed to return to MIT for two final performances, *Antigone* and *Paradise*. This telegram arrived from MIT as the company was about to begin *Mysteries* at Brown:

MIT regretfully must postpone performances of the Living Theatre for both Thursday and Friday evenings. The conclusion of the faculty and the auditorium staff present Tuesday night was that the number of people in the house at the last performance, crowding on stage and in the aisles, was far in excess of legal limits. This condition, together with violation of fire regulations, created a major safety hazard.

The design of the auditorium and your dramatic format are such that control and size of the audience becomes impossible. This could compromise our license.

Since there is no other facility on campus where your company could perform, we are trying to arrange for a suitable theater downtown for a return engagement. If this effort is unsuccessful, we will make full reimbursement according to previous arrangements for each performance. Ticket holders will also be refunded.

It was signed by Professor Richard M. Douglas, head of MIT's Department of Humanities, and by his administrative assistant, Warren A. Seamans. The next morning Julian and road manager Bob Cohen met with Dr. Douglas and other members of the administration. The meeting, which lasted well into the afternoon, indicated cancellation rather than "postponement" of the last two shows, and irate trustees of the Institute were claimed to be the ones behind it all. But what about the second *Antigone?* The first one had drawn a full house without breaching any fire and safety regulations. Evasions and phumpers, and finally the stalemated meeting, were brought to an end by a well-timed phone call from the local chief of police: *Paradise* was banned in Cambridge. And that was that. Well then, did this ban also apply to the city of Boston itself? No one could really say for sure. An alternative theatre was sought, with Boston the area of concentration. Many leads were followed up, but each one led to an impasse, until it was too late; the company had to leave for Goddard College in Vermont.

105

Footnote: In December, just prior to Christmas engagements in New York City, *Paradise* was invited to Boston's John Hancock Hall in the Roxbury section, and this was said to have been its best performance to that date: half the audience-participants were policemen who had come out to bust it. A third Boston engagement took place in March just before the final run at the Brooklyn Academy of Music, but this time *Mysteries* and *Antigone* were presented.

November 20: Castleton State Teachers College . . . The Following Night: Bennington College

A brace of one-night stands in Vermont, about fifty miles and two snow storms apart on a geo-climatic reading . . . and the weather's about as far as they'd get if they ever got together for a seminar, but later. . . . Both nights *Paradise,* making three in a row since Pittsburgh, each one before three completely different audience cross-sections with three completely different reactions, Castleton and Bennington representing the extremes of college life, American style.

Vital information re Castleton State College: Tuition here is $200 a year with a large percentage of the enrollment receiving financial aid to meet that; out-of-state tuition is $1,100, but since it is a state-supported school, Vermonters have top priority. Students are predominantly from low-income, rural, farm backgrounds; others from slate and granite quarrying families. The enrollment is said to be about 1,364; the gymnasium was set up to accommodate 1,500 and it was sold out, many parents as well as some townspeople having

106

come out to see the Living. Only one student was said to be missing that night . . . a girl who had refused to come because she was "afraid of them." This is actually a state *teachers* college, interesting in light of the near-violence and hysteria that greeted the company and its preachments. Statistics regarding Castleton, Vermont are hard to come by . . . World Almanac for 1968 lists only Rutland County . . . but the total population can probably be speculated on the basis of there being only one policeman in town. And he left shortly after the performance began.

With the exception of the police statistic, none of this information had been checked out pre-performance; it trickled into the dressing room as the show was in progress, and we wondered what the hell we were doing in this enclave of Wallace supporters, young fascists, and duck-assed motorcycle freaks. We never did find out what the hell we were doing there, and it was pretty hairy. These kids were scared, up-tight, and to them the Living were all those Commie Fags they'd heard about, Commie Fags out to get Mom and deflower their sisters, move next door and overthrow America. They did go through some changes, though . . . the initial lack of comprehension soared rapidly to frustrated violence, reaching its climax in hysteria, and by the end a mood of hostile fascination had settled in, bringing its own discomforting aura. It was a steady struggle of rock-bound wills, the students lashing out and resisting every possible contact, and the Living going at them relentlessly, shaking them up, *torturing them* simply by being there.

After the show the company was visibly fatigued by the experience. Haggard and seemingly drained of energy, they

107

were preparing to leave when someone came in and told them that he had been advised that no one should walk out to the bus alone. We left the building in small groups and walked through the snow to our bus which was parked in the lot behind the gymnasium. Finally all aboard and ready to go, Tony flicks on the headlights—and there in the shadows next to the building and under the trees, singly or in clusters of two and three, their eyes glazed and staring at the bus, mouths gaped in bovine vacuity, bodies hanging slack and completely disarmed—the most violently threatening young men from the audience. Their minds completely blown by *Paradise*.

Twenty-four hours later, Bennington College, a progressive liberal arts institution for young women . . . and the only women's college on the tour. The current enrollment is about 500 young ladies from predominantly upper to super-upper income families who pay the highest college tuition in the country—$4,000 a year—and few scholarships are available. When I was a student there about twenty percent of the students came from abroad, and the only Vermonters encountered were children enrolled in the campus nursery school where child-psych majors twisted their heads. Over the years Bennington has encampused within its 300 acres (usually described as "rolling") numerous faculty "stars," among them Martha Graham, Howard Nemerov, Wallace Fowlie, and currently Stanley Edgar Hyman and Bernard Malamud. Jackson Pollock, Dylan Thomas, Norman Mailer, and James Baldwin made guest visitations—in the vivid words of Caitlin Thomas, "rousing the Furies in their underpants." The point: Bennington is not to be confused with Castleton.

The point was missed by the Living, the first of such oversights caused by no one's having bothered beforehand to find out where student audiences were at and the differences between certain colleges. At Castleton the actors had eventually succeeded by turning animosity into a reluctant fascination. But the situation here was different, and it was obvious that the troupe had come to depend too heavily on a supposed "mystique," which on closer scrutiny was rooted in an annoying self-satisfaction that concealed laziness and a lack of group discipline. It was so easy to stick to the script, to blow the same riffs, no matter that they didn't happen to apply to the given set of circumstances; *Paradise* was as programmed, as inflexible, as the system it set out to attack. At Bennington it was taken with polite indifference; at Berkeley it would be turned into a full-blown fiasco.

The problem at Bennington was that the audience was on the Living's side out front, an amiable condition that usually makes anarchy gratuitous, but there weren't enough actors who grasped the situation in time to change it. Following the "Rite of Guerilla Theatre" ("I'm not allowed to travel without a passport, I don't know how to stop the wars, etc.") that opens *Paradise,* about a dozen girls and boys had taken off all their clothes and joined the performance. The rest of the spectators (about three hundred people, presumably a perfect number for this show, divided almost equally between female students and male visitors) were amused and

109

undaunted by the "Nervous Nellies" and "stupid cunts" tossed at them by the actors, and one suspected that perhaps the students' interest and curiousity were more intellectual than the proceedings warranted. As it turned out they only resented being *screamed at*.

"Why must you shout at me? Can't you just talk to me?" asked one with a politeness that only served to provoke more rancor from her assailant.

"But I agree with you . . . why are you yelling at me?" demanded another, while others, giving in to female hystrionics, wailed back, "Don't scream at me, you fucking idiot! . . . I don't hate you because you're black. I hate you because you're spitting in my face!"

Those in the company who tried to break with the usual rough tactics eventually dropped out of the performance, got dressed, and joined the girls. They were outnumbered by too many who were determined to create a hostile atmosphere, and ultimately the willfulness of this group exposed certain weaknesses in *Paradise Now* that could easily lead to its rejection as a serious effort to bring about a revolution. Some minor errors in the unadjusted "script" ("How many prisoners are there in the jail in the town of Bennington?" There is no jail in the town of Bennington. "If you paid to get in here, you got screwed!" Students had not paid to attend the performance) made it merely theatrical; it must be a play because they don't know what they're talking about. Later, having hurriedly been briefed that this was not the typical girls' school they might have expected, one or two of the actors expressed a certain resentment against students whose family wealth assured them an academic

110

freedom that should be the right of students everywhere. There is little question of the validity of this opinion, but unfortunately an actor expressed this resentment by slapping a girl across the face during a heated confrontation. This same girl had previously taken part in one of the body piles; what further proof is needed that she had been in accord with the Living and, from the standpoint of participation beyond the call of duty, wasn't *all* bad? She left the performance in tears, and others who remained, myself included, were very disturbed and put off by the incident.

This wasn't the first incident of an actor slapping a spectator. At a performance of *Mysteries* at the Brooklyn Academy of Music, a girl had come onstage to goose-around with Gene Gordon as he stood motionless in the spotlight at the very beginning of the show. She had poked and groped and pulled his hair, and finally, unable to dislodge him, she rammed against him and knocked him off balance. Regaining his balance, he then slapped her and returned to his immobile position. Startled, the girl turned to the audience and cried, "Isn't anyone going to help a lady?" Either because they thought she was part of the show or because they didn't think she was a lady, no one came forward and the show continued without further interference. Some people who knew she wasn't part of the show had been upset by Gordon's action, arguing (naïvely, it seemed to me) that if the Living Theatre was nonviolent, how come he hit her? As far as I was concerned, Gordon's action was perfectly defensible. That chick had no business onstage at that point in *Mysteries;* she was just another wise-ass in search of attention, and Gordon had done what any normal, red-blooded freak would have done under those circumstances. But now, after all the chaos and near-violence that had been dealt with on other occasions—at Yale, at the Brooklyn Academy of Music, at Castleton the night before—to hit a girl at a "girls' school"? In the dressing room afterward the actor had gotten a severe blast from others in the company who had also been disturbed by the incident, but when it had happened, his action had further alienated the company from its audience—the first time to this date that they had been alienated *by* an audience.

At the party after the performance the only outsiders in attendance were a small committee of students who served the food, and writer Claude Fredricks, a faculty member and long-time friend of the Becks who had produced his play *The Idiot King* in 1954. For a college with a very strong emphasis on the performing arts, this wasn't the warmest welcome for an important theatrical event.

November 24–26: YM-YWHA, Philadelphia

"I'd rather be here than in Philadelphia."
Epitaph on tombstone of W. C. Fields

The Philadelphia YM-YWHA has, according to members of its Arts Council, a reputation for avant-garde cultural things —the Alwin Nikolais and Paul Taylor dance companies, Edward Albee before *Virginia Woolf,* Nico and the Velvet Underground. *The Brig* was done there when the Living Theatre was still in New York, and this was the first place in Philadelphia to have an exhibition of Pop Art. The

112

policy, expressed by a lady of the Council, has something to do with exposing people to what's happening so they can form their own opinions, to give them the opportunity to Grasp It Now. Good-o. . . .

The final performance; *Paradise* is up for grasps. Somehow it has attracted a heavy hair-piece-false-eyelash contingent escorted by men in adaptations of Mod drag, and as could be expected, the local hippies and "heads" of the community are out, too, all hanging in with a sort of ecstatic apathy that's hard to find in most places. Meanwhile, onstage, an elderly Jewish man is putting Julian down for not taking power for the Jews, the most intelligent people in the world, he says, and so on; an incredible Jewish riff, for a change, and for some reason—maybe it's the vaguely maniacal expression on his face—you have the impression that Julian's trying not to break up. When he's finally able to get in a word, Julian tries to say that this man's point of view is similar to that of the Nazis who oppressed the Jews, and he mentions that there are concentration camps today in Israel. Both parties carry on belligerently, until the man calls Julian a "fink Jew," and pointing to his (Julian's) loincloth, he yells, "You're only wearing that because you're ashamed to show your circumcision! You don't even know the Kabala!" Julian cracks up and walks away, and another actor approaches the raving man and says, "Excuse me, are you Jewish?"

In the lobby, a pregnant lady is saying good-night to the Arts Council ladies. She insists that she's not feeling well, but she looks as if she'll be zooming around as soon as she gets the hell out of *Paradise*. In parting she says, "Do call us if you need us." The ladies giggle, but she repeats it *in italics* and turns to catch up with her husband who's already at the elevator. Later it turns out that her husband is the assistant D.A. It also turns out later, when such things will prove convenient, that the full-D.A. is a trustee of the Y and was at the performance.

The Philadelphia Troubles

The auditorium was on the third floor of the building, and when some of us were able to get down the crowded staircase to the main lobby, there was a noisy crush of people, mostly young people, around the entrance. There were a couple of policemen standing in the lobby, slightly behind the crowd that jammed the doors. There was some sort of commotion there, but probably because the cops in the lobby didn't appear to be paying very much attention to it, I assumed that it was just a crowd of noisy kids exhilarated by the show they had just seen, joining the exiting crowd. . . .

I hear shouts from the street where several squad cars and paddywagons are now visible from inside the lobby, and suddenly the two cops who had been standing in the rear of the lobby begin to push their way through, shoving people against each other as they ram through the mob. The commotion is much louder now, screams and shouting, and the police on the sidewalk outside of the entrance rush forward and shove the whole middle section of the crowd back, away from the front doors, into the foyer that has several marble steps leading up to a second set of glass doors into the lobby. Thrown off balance by the steps, the people fall backward in waves, falling all the way up the steps and spilling into the lobby. From the edge of the screaming crowd in the foyer, wedged between a wall and the second set of glass doors, I can see a few of the Living, in their loincloths and bikinis, running through the lobby and up the stairs to the dressing rooms. The police grabbed them, but in the turmoil they have managed to get away and are running upstairs to warn the others; most of the company, in fact, went to the dressing rooms when the show ended and don't know what is happening down in the street.

The mob is less violent now. Patrol cars and police are still there and some arrests have been made, but no one is sure how many or who has been arrested. A man from a legal aid organization is asking for the name and address of anyone who has witnessed or been subjected to any police brutality, and in the doorway Bob Cohen is asking to see those who have witnessed the arrests of members of the company. There is much confusion here, because many of those whose arrests were witnessed have also been seen escaping by other witnesses. The only thing certain is that Julian has been arrested and is en route to the station house.

At the station, police refuse to give us any information. How many have been taken? Who are they? Where are they? No answers. Only surly remarks and a threat to arrest Bill Shari who asks the questions. Finally we are told that the arrested will be arraigned in Magistrates Court "sometime tonight."

Magistrates Court: The police seem a bit uncomfortable; as if knowing their function, they are secretly embarrassed by not knowing how to fulfill it; harassment is the best way

115

of asserting their officiality until instructions are handed down. No coffee in the building. Go outside with it. No, you have to stay inside. But don't bring that coffee, you'll deface the building. Stand here, not there. Only one at a time permitted, etc., etc., etc.

Surely they must be insane. But ultimately it is their physical presence that causes the situation to snap its brittle brace on reality, that causes it to lodge itself in hallucination that drifts backward to vernacular actuality. They are sausaged into dingy gray uniforms . . . legs inappropriate to the heft of the bodies . . . fat-white-ham-arms stub out of short sleeves . . . bristly crew cuts . . . bloated vacuous faces with beady . . . pig eyes. Pig eyes. Pig. There is greater respect for the privacy of madmen ("Don't bother him—he's crazy." "Don't talk to that nut.") than for those who, knowing that the odds of belief aren't in their favor, still demand a hearing ("Listen to me. Now I know you won't believe this, but . . .."). If the circumstances warranted it, I wouldn't hesitate to plead insanity to be left in peace, but others have commented on the singularly porcine similitude of these particular lawmen, and weeks later in the course of an informal lecture before a group of students in Ann Arbor, Julian happened to mention the Philadephia engagement. As I recall now, its context was different, but within the mnemonic thread of what he was saying, it came out that he, too, had undergone a similar "hallucination" that night in Philadelphia. His was more appropriately environed, experienced as it was amid the reek and squalor of his cell beneath the double-circle architectonics of the ultramodern building.

Eventually three lawyers arrive to defend the arrested,

and the harassment stops. Judith, five or six of the Living, Cohen, a man from the Arts Council of the "Y," some young people who had attended the show—we are left alone to sit, to stand, to sleep. To wait. Drunken driving. Drunken driving. A trio of go-go dancers from a girlie show and some motley males, busted for some reasons having to do with obscenity. We wait more than five hours for the arraignment of Julian, Steve ben Israel, Hans Schano (alias "Echnaton"), and two people who had been in the audience, one of them a student who, before his courtroom appearance, had to be taken to a hospital for treatment of a wrist injury said to have been caused by handcuffs. It is Wednesday dawn, November 27, when all five are released on nominal bail of one dollar. *Friday, November 29:* the hearing. The first charge of indecent exposure is dismissed in each case. Julian is found guilty on the second charge, inciting a riot.

He is fined five dollars.[1]

---

[1]Footnote on the police: "It's not paranoid to be paranoid anymore," someone had said in another context, but his observation is just as pertinent here. Throughout the trip there were always the police, a third presence that mingled among the audience or stood at attention in the streets beyond. New Haven, MIT, Philadelphia, Cincinnati, Boulder, Chicago, LA, and Berkeley (not in New York because they were on strike during the first Brooklyn run), driving through Kansas, at a Howard Johnson's stop in who-knows-where; the threat implied or the presence at work.

Waiting, watching, expecting what? Hoping for what? And now and then, bored with the waiting and the hoping, it took the initiative and came at you in funny ways that revealed a horrible frustration that could not be eased: in a Detroit diner I am poked by a cop who calls me "faggot." And for some crazy reason you still wonder where the fuck their heads are at.

117

December 6: Cincinnati, Ohio

The Kempler Lane Hotel was undoubtedly a luxury establishment in the days of the great Cincinnati boom, which, as booms go, didn't make too much of a dent in recorded history . . . just sort of clearing the air for the great Covington, Kentucky boom across the river . . . and in its musty decadence, the Kempler Lane stands as the residential embodiment of the expression "to have seen better days." Its semi-circular driveway curves up to a lobby in which furniture is arranged facing the entrance . . . chairs and settees in a sagging Maginot Line on which elderly belles with crimped "perms" sit umbilicused to fierce pekes and outraged cockers, all digging the world beyond the glass doors and getting the daily rundown on what's wrong with it, prime complaints being that there's not enough heat and the maid hasn't vacuumed it yet.

It is late afternoon and the sun's rays have gingerly picked their way through the dusty potted plants and bleached the back-dates a bit paler, when out at the curb the Big Bus pulls up. Its doors snap open and out they march, single file up the driveway—hair thrashing in the wind, velvet capes flapping around guitar cases and sacks of macrobiotic rice, last week's blankets in djellaba reincarnations, the bedspread collection, un-napped children irritable and screaming in their funky furs. The alarm has been sounded, the lobby's a-roil. Good God—*transients!*

Meanwhile, the disembarkment having begun at the curb, a spade midget with a hunchback happens to be ambling down the street. He is wearing a pork-pie hat with a little

118

feather in the band and a brown suit, the jacket of which trails on the sidewalk below his fingertips and rises in back to arch tautly across his hump. Suddenly looking up, he is instantly transfixed and catches a side-view of the panorama at an eye-level of about three feet high. And he just stands there scratching his head. Probably getting a friendly vibration, siphoned in on a radar beam, he tucks in line.

And inside, the crimped ladies are numbed to their seats when in strolls the midget, who can't believe it either, but the ladies *know* he's got to be part of it—they're *all* freaks, all *undesirables,* they've just got to be together. THIS! In MY lobby!!

A straight Gidean flip-out; the watcher watching the watched being watched. And the crimped ladies having spasms, palpitations . . . fumbling for their *medications.* And the spade midget is just standing on the sidelines . . . scratching his head.

December 11: Ann Arbor, Michigan

Brief mention of *Paradise* having its best American performance here. "Best" in terms of coming closest to duplicating the serious acceptance and the atmosphere of spiritual appreciation that had attended some of the European performances—the other side of the equally serious but violent receptions in Geneva and Avignon that got the most coverage. Involved in effecting their own scholastic and political revolutions, the students here responded in a way that made this *Paradise* exceptional.

December 17: University of Rochester, New York State

On arrival in Rochester for one night of *Paradise,* it is learned that a local FM radio station has announced the intention of local authorities to arrest the Living if the performance goes on. In an effort to prevent the incident before it should take place, the Becks pay an afternoon visit to the local precinct. The chief of police is at home bedridden with flu, but three assistants are on hand to hear what they have to say. The Becks speak calmly of their troupe's pacifistic tenets, emphasizing the nonviolent, the spiritual, the creative intent of the show; they admit that it does attract a fairly large turn-out, but being accustomed to this sort of thing, the company manages to keep things pretty much under control, peaceful, nonviolent, creative.

The officers warm up to them and admit it is just that the local press has called their attention to this matter, has gotten them upset, a bit concerned . . . perhaps overly so, but then, in effect, "We only know what we read in the newspapers."

Oh, for goodness sakes, say the Becks, surely you must know better than to accept everything you read in the newspapers. "Just look what they say about the police," muses Julian.

December 24–31: Poe Forum, New York

Actually the less said about this engagement the better; however, it is useful to explain how the Living Theatre happened

120

to get booked into this dilapidated ex-moviehouse in the Bronx when just a few weeks ago three Broadway theatres had been offered for a limited Christmas holiday engagement.

The Broadway offers had been rejected out front by the Becks and by those of the company who tend to follow through with the same shop-worn dialectic that holds that Broadway is the enemy, dialectic that would be resurrected again when Broadway's ANTA Theatre was offered for the final performances before leaving the States; it would have a more important bearing on the circumstances then.

Having turned down Broadway for Christmas, the next possibility in New York was the Fillmore East, which had ungraciously hosted the Up Against The Wall Theatre Benefit in October. Despite the much-publicized participation of the Living in the "occupation" which had mercifully terminated the benefit, a Fillmore run was quite conceivable. In early November Saul Gottlieb was enlisted to find a non-Broadway house for the holidays. Possibly afraid to deal with the Fillmore's Bill Graham after the benefit-occupation incident, Gottlieb failed to follow this up, putting it off until it was too late to book a decent theatre anywhere in the city. As a result, the holiday season set in, and the Living returned to New York for a "special" engagement at the only place available: the Poe Forum in the Bronx, a filthy, cavernous hall with neither heat nor dressing rooms. It also happened that, having been a moviehouse in an earlier life, it lacked a proper stage for live presentations. On the afternoon before the first performance workmen were hurriedly trying to remedy this deficiency, while actors sat around

121

waiting to erect the *Frankenstein* set as soon as a stage was erected on which to put it.

But that Sunday a deferential reporter for the *New York Times* fairly burbles with joy as she tells how the Radical Theatre Repertory is helping to bring about the revolution. Saul Gottlieb comes on with a quoted indulgence to the effect that booking the Living Theatre into the Poe Forum is a well-calculated tactical maneuver: Why not start the revolution in the Bronx? (or something like that). The whole number is such a *folie a deux* that it should have been captioned "All the Fits It's News to Print," but instead it's capped by the startling revelation that Mr. Gottlieb is "the impresario of the emerging radical theatre movement." This refers to the new theatre groups, most of which have been around for several years. But if this statement is true, the new theatre is, to paraphrase *Paradise,* in a state of "emergency" and doesn't even know it.

After this grind, three performances at Hunter College before leaving New York for Chicago. The Gateway to the West, someone said.

Antigone

The Hölderlin translation of the Sophocles play into German appeared in 1804; in 1948 Bertolt Brecht's adaptation had its world premiere in Switzerland. While faithful to the poetic feeling of the Hölderlin text, Brecht deleted its precepts of divinity and situated it firmly within the secular and political consciousness of man. Brecht's *Antigone* underscores the individual's moral sensibility in conflict with that of the masses who have relinquished control and become sycophants to a tyrannical and unjust leader. One of the most germane and direct reflections of the political tenets of the Living Theatre, this text depicts the malignancies afflicting a social order that is already established. It is the step beyond *Frankenstein*, but where that suggests a peaceful alternative to the cyclical tolerance of political oppression, *Antigone* concludes with the total destruction of man through tyranny. In connecting the two works in terms of theatrical impact and content, it could be said that *Frankenstein* is an explosion, a dense assemblage that is essentially visceral in effect; *Antigone* is the containment of that force, an implosion in which the physical dynamics function through the unparalleled plasticity with which it is conceived and staged.

Though less overwhelming in theatrical presence, less imposing in physical appearance, this is pure deception; *Antigone* approaches *Frankenstein* as a masterwork in the art of the Living Theatre. Others may perform it, but *Antigone* will never be done as the Living Theatre does it.

In 1961 Judith Malina began the English translation of Brecht's *Antigone*. Hers is a complete reconstruction of the text, set in free verse form in order to maintain word-for-word precision, and in translating the passages created by Brecht, she has tried to preserve his poetic meter as accurately as possible in English. In the Living's production, directed by Judith, Brecht's spoken prologue is replaced by a sound-and-movement piece, but with the exception of some very minor changes, the entire text is presented. *Antigone* was an experiment to find out if the Artaudian devices were possible with a text that was poetic, political, and classical in origin, though contemporary in application.

In directing it, Judith retained the Brechtian device of having an actor step out of character to outline the action in advance to the audience. Aside from imparting a Brechtian handle, the purpose of preserving this element in an avant-garde production of a modern adaptation of a classical play was threefold: (1) to challenge the actors with a more formal dramatic condition; (2) to show that the Brechtian techniques could also be applied in the Artaud-oriented framework of the company; and (3) because these bridge lines, delivered by the actors in a straightforward, deadpan style, would have a very practical use—translated into French, German, Italian, Spanish, and Serbo-Croatian, these

124

would be the only lines spoken in the language of the audience. The rest of the play would be performed in English.

With the elimination of Brecht's prologue, the play begins as the spectators are filing into their seats. Both house-lights and stage-lights are on. Slowly the actors appear onstage and stand facing the audience, their eyes staring with frigid animosity directly into the faces of the spectators. On guard and threatening, they begin a resonant drone, a breath that passes through the nasal passages; the mouths are closed and still. Groups form briefly and then separate as they move about in an atmosphere of tension and hostility, unsettling the audience and sizing it up; as the spectators increase, the number of actors onstage increases proportionately until both sides have settled in and are ready for action. The relationship is established; it is a state of war. The audience is the enemy Argos; the stage is Thebes. The droning respiration has risen to a disquieting siren-like wail . . . an actor screams and falls to his knees, his arms protecting his head; this is repeated by others. The wail persists as Creon sends troops into Argos. The theatre is lighted until the battle ends. Silence. The house-lights go off. Antigone (Judith Malina) enters with Ismene; the dialogue begins.

Antigone is performed on a bare stage. The actors, all of whom remain in the action either on stage or in the theatre, are dressed in dark colored shirts and pants, without jewelry or other adornment, and most are barefoot. All sounds are produced from the actors' voices and bodies; the action is pantomimed and "props" (the war machines, Creon's throne, Tiresias' chair, Antigone's cell, and the "Bosch machines"—contorted configurations that symbolize the infirmity of the state) are formed by the bodies of the actors.

When Brecht removed *Antigone* from the Sophoclean sphere of divinity and gave it a political interpretation, two basic themes developed which in the Living Theatre's production gain astonishing dimension because of their particular relevance to the political climate of today. *To set an example* is one of the motifs: Antigone defies Creon's (Julian Beck) law and tries to rouse the people to take action to put an end to the debilitating war he has perpetuated against Argos. In so doing, she commits an act of civil disobedience and is imprisoned by Creon, who must silence her if his despotic reign is to continue. Knowing that her death may arouse the suspicion of the populace, he tries to persuade her that her beliefs are wrong, that it is useless to oppose him. When this fails, he then tries to convince his supporters that she is mad, a tactic which is more effective, since as is the case with all tyrants, Creon is in symbiotic collusion with the lesser officials whose ambition and self-seeking are best served by acquiesence. This is symbolized in the play by his speaking from the center of configurations formed by the Thebans, by his being carried (supported) by them; when moving independently he limps. He does not move too far away from his supporters; they never leave him alone too long. They are all threatened by Antigone's altruism, by her example which, were it to be followed by the people, would bring the collapse of their rule.

126

Antigone is not portrayed as a revolutionary heroine, but rather as a woman whose action is motivated by moral consciousness. She disobeys Creon because he is a human law, and human beings can break it. "Man's destiny is man" is the Brechtian premise on which this is based, and as such, human laws must be broken when they set out to repress and destroy the natural destiny of man, when they are not in harmony with man's moral sensibility. In burying her brother Polyneices, whom Creon has ordered to be left unburied because he had opposed Creon and was killed fighting with the enemy Argos against Thebes, Antigone goes only as far as sprinkling dust over his corpse to hide it from the vultures. It is a symbolic act that has its parallel in much of today's nonviolent protest that questions the legal interpretation of *unwritten laws;* it confuses authorities and provokes reprisals (or, in the words of Mayor Daley, "an over-reaction") that would also be analogous to those of Creon and his supporters.

Through this symbolic expression of her intentions, Antigone establishes a situation that tests the power of Creon and exposes his weaknesses; however, it is too late to save Thebes. The second theme is that of *too late:* Antigone acts *too late;* Ismene, Hemon, Tiresias, *too late;* the people listen *too late.* They turn away from Creon and realize that Thebes, already decimated by Creon's war with Argos, now faces extermination by the enemy; the tragedy is confronted *too late.*

The Living Theatre premiered *Antigone* on February 19, 1967 in Krefeld, Germany. Bill Shari played the part of

127

Tiresias, the blind seer whose warning of destruction is ignored by Creon and the Thebans. After the first few performances, Bill Shari became ill and was unable to work for a while and in his absence Rufus Collins, one of the Negro actors, took the role. This replacement was intended as a temporary measure; however, it was to remain a permanent change even after Shari had recovered. The role of Tiresias had accidentally assumed a new meaning when played by a Negro, a meaning that may not have been as striking in Europe as it was in America. For as the play itself became more dimensioned through its relevance to the political dissent in America, the part of Tiresias took on special significance as the black voice that tries to alert a complacent nation that its complicity with oppression can only end in catastrophe. As the blind seer who is black, Tiresias becomes the ancient race that is kept in darkness, whose wisdom springs from the primitive instinct for sensing danger. The Dance of Bacchus has begun when Tiresias enters. He is led by a child: the young bringing forth the transcendental sensibility of a primitive culture.

Tiresias warns Creon and the Elders (the majority), but his words are a discomforting bring-down that interrupts the festivities, the celebration ordered by Creon to assure his people that nothing is wrong, that his war will be won. The blind seer, the black Tiresias' words are ignored. And the dance goes on.

January 7–12: University of Chicago

Despite a certain apprehension about playing in Chicago, this turned out to be the most interesting city so far. The first city in quite some time to even qualify as such, it had much to offer those able to take advantage of it, but for most of the company, mobility being restricted both by the limited number of vehicles at their disposal and by the inadequate public transportation facilities of the city itself, Chicago was just another city, only larger than most. In light of the bloodshed and violence surrounding the Democratic Convention, plus the explosive conditions in the ghettoes that girdled it, Chicago was potentially a far more hazardous venture than other places, but as far as the Living Theatre's performances were concerned, this terrible potential was not fulfilled.

What made this engagement significant was the change in *Paradise Now,* a long overdue modification resulting from serious efforts to tighten it up and make it more effective. It should have been done much earlier in the tour, but there always seemed to be reasons, or excuses, for postponing it. I think that it was finally brought about now because of the sensate pressures of being in this particular place with this particular show. The usual procedure was for the company to get together an hour or so before the performance and go over whatever information had to be fitted in that dealt with the community where the show was to take place. Most of the time this was done hurriedly in the dressing room beforehand, and there was usually too much other business to take care of at the same time (who was sick and couldn't play, their lines to be taken by others; important announcements, changes in schedule). But in Chicago an entire afternoon had been devoted to a meeting at which representatives of a number of local liberal and radical factions had been present to brief the company on the civic condition and how it affected . . . disaffected . . . the people. When the guests had left, the rest of the day was spent discussing and debating the ways in which *Paradise Now* would be made relevant to Chicago.

In terms of initial hostility and tumult, the show that night wasn't terribly different from so many others, but there was a major difference: the command the company had of themselves and, therefore, of the audience. By limiting the amount of time allotted for the confrontations with members of the audience (the "actions"), the level of tension was raised and a new excitement was created. Another difference was in the large percentage of older people who stayed for the whole show—an observation which in the context of an earlier criticism concerning the necessity of trying to reach an older audience may have contributed to the quality of this *Paradise*. This isn't meant to imply that *Paradise* could be mistaken for a community sing . . . screaming, shouting, hysteria, and tension, the usual verbal flagellation

130

from all sides . . . so from this standpoint it was the same old show that often seems like a reversal of *Frankenstein* where the spectators are being garroted, hanged, shot, and otherwise "victimized." But the lengthy afternoon meeting had wrought a serious change, and by its mid-point not only had much of the hostility given way to less random confrontations, but an almost reverential mood had set in, and by finish it proved to be a particularly good performance, comparable to the one in Ann Arbor, but a more exciting conquest of a really challenging circumstance.

It should also be noted that in the tightening-up and tucking-in process, *Paradise Now* was now at least a half-hour shorter than its original four-hour-plus duration: another major victory. On January 24 the Living was invited back for one *Paradise* at the Chicago Civic Center, an auditorium that accommodates close to three thousand people. This was known in advance to be far too many people for a successful show, but at least this one, too, was pulled off without incident.

January 15–16: Madison, Wisconsin

Because of a problem in obtaining a police permit for Turner Hall, the two performances scheduled to go on there (*Antigone* and *Paradise;* the permit was refused because of the latter) were switched to a Unitarian church designed by Frank Lloyd Wright and conveniently implanted three miles outside of Madison. The chapel provided a dramatic, if crowded, environment for *Antigone* and things went well. However, the following night began with a church official's unexpected announcement that the Unitarian church wasn't responsible for having invited the Living Theatre to Madison, and a further elaboration came with his explanation that this space had merely been "lent" after Turner Hall had proved unavailable for the performances. He wound up by declaring, very clearly and in a tone somewhat louder than before, that his church would not be responsible for anything that happened during the performance of *Paradise Now.* Applause. Giggles. *Paradise* begins . . . .

But before it ends the minister has unceremoniously fled his flock in total outrage: among the throngs of exuberant spectators were two young ladies who had jackknifed off of his cantilevered pulpit—stark naked.

The following morning, Friday, January 17: We are preparing to leave Madison for Appleton, Wisconsin, about three hours north as the buses go. To digress for a moment, the remains of the late Senator Joseph McCarthy are resting-presumably-in-peace in Appleton, Wisconsin, its other dubious achievement being that it was also his birthplace. Suffice it to say that *Paradise* and *Antigone* weren't the two shows presented there.

In any event, we are preparing to set out from Madison when it is brought to everyone's attention that the Radical Theatre Repertory has neglected to send money to pay the company. Naturally this causes a mild ripple which is instantly manifest in frantically criss-crossing phone calls (collect) to the producers in New York, specifically to Saul Gottlieb, who supposedly claims that due to having paid a few thousand dollars ($7,000 was the figure quoted as having come from Gottlieb) in income taxes on the tour's earnings for that quarter, he is unable to meet the payroll this week. This strikes me as a piously perverse reason to give the Living Theatre for hanging up the salaries, but it also bears the earmarkings of a lie: the tax money was supposed to have already been on hand. A few more calls result in the wiring of enough money to pay the hotel bills, and it is arranged for the balance of the salaries to be paid from the Appleton receipts the following night.

Whenever Julian had been in New York, lawyers and accountants, close friends, and a couple of actors in the company had tried to warn him that the farther the tour progressed from New York, the more the dangers would increase for this sort of thing to happen. Before leaving in January on

134

the westward leg, they had tried once again to get Julian to limit the control of the Radical Theatre Repertory, namely Gottlieb, over his company's finances. Julian had always agreed that this was necessary and had promised to take steps to see that it was done, either by himself or by the two or three in the company who had managed these matters in Europe. There seemed to be no question of Julian's having been made fully aware of the internecine conflicts between those at the production end. It wasn't that he was incapable of taking action: it was more as if he couldn't be bothered; having transcended the immediate reality, it was as if these problems were accepted as "inevitabilities" whose course should not be altered . . . it was the price one paid for dealing with the System . . . and yet he made but negligible, perfunctory attempts to manipulate his own system that would benefit those dependent upon him, those of the Living Theatre. Like a visionary with little foresight, he reacted in emergencies when it was too late to change the course of adversity, and eventually those who had assumed these responsibilities in Europe gave up in disappointment.

In a way, they had no choice but to drop out and stay on the sidelines watching, because authority was so diffusely delegated that communications were limited and inaccurate: an odd situation for a group of people so intent upon communication, so aware of the need for meaningful contact between people, and seemingly so capable of communicating to others. But here, the road managers were the liaisons with New York, often the "runners" among the company itself, and until a situation was inflated to calamity, information filtered back and forth via them. For the most part the

135

road managers were another problem, qualifications in this particular case being almost impossible to fulfill: they would have to be experienced, competent and honest when it came to business; they would have to be the sort of hip squares who could get along with the Living, yet be diplomatically cool enough to deal with deans, theatre managers, fire marshals and countless other irate citizens. Such creatures did not report for duty at the Radical office. The first road manager, a friend of Living from its New York days, stayed until the closing night in New Haven, during which he absconded with $800 given him by Gottlieb to pay the hotel bills. His embezzlement could have been condoned on the grounds that the Radical Theatre Repertory had not paid his salary for the two weeks that he had been in its employ, but it *was* a huge drag when everyone was locked out of their rooms until Yale agreed to send over money to cover the bills. He did get a lot of mileage out of the money, though; Spain and North Africa, and back in time to catch the shows at the Poe Forum. The second road manager, another Radical Theatre Repertory discovery but not as jet-setty as the first one, lacked just about all the qualifications for the job, but compensated by staying stoned most of the time. Only the third one came close to fulfilling the perfect road manager fantasy, and paradoxically, it was his complete integrity that in the end played a small and blameless part in helping to fuck things up.

But here they are in Madison with no money on payday, waiting for money to be wired to bail them out of the hotel. This was the opening quiver of the quake that would finally burst in California.

136

After Chicago: Madison, Appleton, two shows in Iowa City (State University of Iowa), back to Chicago for one *Paradise*, then on again—Kansas City; Hays, Kansas; Fort Collins, Colorado; four days in Boulder and on to Portland. A general mood of fatigue has set in and everyone appears drained from the dreary migration. Many are sick with flu, colds, and the remnants of bronchial ailments contracted in the high altitudes of Boulder, and it's probably just the vague anticipation of California, The End, in a sense, that keeps us going.

137

February 11–15: Portland, Oregon

The Living was here for four performances at nearby Reed College, a purpose soon to be overshadowed by two disagreeable developments. The first occurred in New York and had no direct effect on the company until later when those whose help was needed abandoned it to fend for itself against old friend Saul Gottlieb and his Radical Theatre Repertory. Word reached Portland that Gottlieb had stabbed Mel Howard and injured Howard's two secretaries and the elevator operator who had delivered the raging Gottlieb to Howard's office. Gottlieb's fury was apparently provoked by a check from one of the colleges that had been sent to Howard instead of to the RTR, and Howard had refused to turn the check, which amounted to about $1,400, over to the RTR. But having run up a phone bill of $1,100, and being two weeks in arrears for the rental of the company bus, Gottlieb was desperate for money.

Exactly how Gottlieb was spending the profits on the Living Theatre tour was something of a mystery. The other groups listed on his numerous mailers and brochures as being members of his Repertory weren't receiving whatever benefits were supposedly due them as part of the "sponsoring organization"—which may be explicable, since most of them disclaimed any such alliance—and the reasons offered for the monies' disappearance usually turned out to be untrue. Whenever the accountants representing the other producers demanded to see the RTR ledgers, Gottlieb either cancelled these appointments at the last minute or "forgot" the books when he did appear. Once or twice he or his wife, Oda, did show their accounts to the others but they were so badly organized and itemized that they were practically useless. To compound this, road manager Cohen's accounting was said to be in equal disorder and frequently weeks behind in arrival to New York. The actual financial situation appeared to be hopelessly entangled, and about the only readily available evidence was the RTR office, a fairly large apartment in New York's East Village, which also served as the residence of the resourceful Gottliebs, and which had as many as twelve people employed to handle the nebulous business of the RTR. Gottlieb himself was on the payroll as "press agent" for the Living Theatre, and Oda was listed as his assistant or "coordinator," and they gave themselves weekly salaries of $200 apiece for their respective malfunctions.

In the wake of his attack on Howard, charges were brought against Gottlieb and he was released on $500 bail pending the court hearing. He jumped bail by flying to California to "help" the company out of its troubles there, but Howard dropped the charges at the hearing, mainly to avoid the publicity that would probably ensue, but also because of the zeal with which the Gottliebs spread Their Side of the incident: Gottlieb was becoming a "martyr" among his misguided self-styled following of "radicals" who seemed to feel

140

that stabbing someone and injuring others wasn't nice—after all, it was violent—but on the other hand, calling the police to break it up was horrendous. Old radicals are really too fucking much.

In Portland Mark Amitin was waiting, for what wasn't clear even to Mark himself. As the only employee of the RTR with any real competence and capability, Mark had worked diligently out of the New York office, and Gottlieb had sent him to California to arrange the West Coast bookings. He had been on the coast for several weeks now, taking care of the advance sales, publicity, and hotel arrangements, and everything would appear to be in order, except that in all that time Mark had received no salary from New York. He had been using his own rapidly dwindling savings for business expenses and for the small amount of publicity they could be stretched to cover. He had borrowed from friends and relatives in California to supplement expenses that were Gottlieb's responsibility, and at this point he was in debt for more than what was owed him in back salary. To say the least, Mark's devotion to the Living was a bit naïve, but it was nice to have someone conscientious in charge for a change.

He had come to Portland just to see that everything was all right, but really to see the company, bedraggled as it was, and in a funny way his cheerful presence was a reassurance that California did exist, torrential rain, mudslides, and all. No one foresaw the more immediate disasters that would pour down on the Living, but for me, just getting to California was enough—it would finally end the frustration of plodding across the map state by state.

141

The second problem: no salaries. Accompanied by the recurrent nemesis: hotel bills. The salaries had to be put off until the next stop, Ashland, in order to pay the nemesis in full and get the Living the hell out of Portland. Gottlieb had commandeered the check from Reed College.

February 16: Ashland, Oregon

. . . a thoroughly forgettable college town where we did one *Antigone* and two nights. By now you hesitate to bring your luggage into the motel, fearing that it might be locked in when you think you're checking out.

Flashback to somewhere between Kansas City and Boulder, I think: Broadway's ANTA Theatre had invited the Living Theatre to perform in the final three weeks of the tour. This would necessitate flying the company back east after California, but at his point, most would have been willing to get off the bus by any means possible. The contractual agreements offered by ANTA would have included a five-figure advance against box office receipts plus a percentage of the profits thereafter that could have sent them back to Europe with an even healthier five- or six-figure stake. The shows could have been arranged in any way the company decided to present them, with *Paradise,* the biggest moneymaker, understood to be given the most performances. However, Julian chose to consider this as a booking of sixteen *Paradises,* or at least that was the emphasis given when the proposal was placed before the company, and apparently on those grounds it had been rejected, exhaustion having set in long before Portland.

But now it's Ashland, Oregon, and there's no money. Rufus and Gianfranco decide to try to reach Mel Howard, through whom the ANTA proposal had come, and find out if it was still possible to accept it in the event that Julian could be persuaded to change his mind. Howard isn't home. Carl Einhorn and Mark Amitin are brought into the consultation, the money situation is reviewed, and, still unable to reach Howard in New York, a decision is reached to take action in the meantime. A call is placed to the RTR office and Oda answers, explaining that Saul is "busy" on another phone and can't talk to them, and she is informed of the circumstances; the company needs x-thousands of dollars to cover salaries and pay for the buses until the end, and for the return to Europe.[1] Other incidentals are mentioned . . . for example, the money from the CBS-TV show, taped in October and telecast January 12, still hadn't been paid to the actors by the RTR through which CBS had paid for the performance . . . and Oda is told that since all of the California contracts are in Mark Amitin's name, the proceeds will go directly to the company and be held until its expenses are paid. Naturally this precipitates a mild furor on the New York end of the wire. Oda threatens to go to Equity and collect the bond; she is told to go ahead and try, warned of the consequences this act would have on the tour; viz., it would end, which is what everyone wants by now, and on this note the call is terminated.

---

[1]By the expiration date of Michael Butler's guarantee, $4,000 had been paid by Gottlieb, and this was being held by the travel agent as a deposit on the return fares. A balance of $6,000 was still owed.

144

Julian is then asked to join the meeting and justify his refusal to go on Broadway, and he agrees to do so. Others come to the room, but most drift in and stay long enough to make comment which is either irrelevant or a parroting of what has just been said, usually by Julian. It's hardly the sort of attention one would expect in a crisis, and its tone is set when Julian opens by saying that money is a repulsive reason for wanting to take the company on Broadway. Rufus and Gianfranco sympathize, but seem to feel that perhaps vulgarity ought to be overlooked for the sake of factual evidence. Julian elaborates on his anti-Broadway viewpoint. There are many people traveling with them who very much want to join the company. He had considered the Broadway question on the condition that the Living Theatre be divided in half for the *Paradise* shows (which he insists will total sixteen); this would permit those who wanted to play on Broadway to do so, and those opposed, along with those non-member participants, could give free performances elsewhere, perhaps guerilla theatre pieces in the streets or in various locations around the city, while the Broadway show was being done.

But on further consideration, he and Judith had rejected this idea, because to play Broadway at all would be selling out, it would be fortifying the Broadway System by allowing it to contain the Living Theatre; that System would then be able to boast of its broadmindedness, its flexibility. We can even absorb the contempt of the Living Theatre, it would say, and the Living Theatre would be the court jesters to the Broadway bourgeoisie who could pay $10 a seat to be insulted in the name of culture. He declared that he would not

145

be able to face his fellow man-on-the-street in honest confrontation knowing that he had sold out to Broadway. He couldn't live with himself after that.

Rufus argues that it would be a meaningful ending for the American tour, that it would be a frontal attack on bourgeois values in their own bastions. So far the other alternative is a moviehouse on 14th Street; it will be another Poe Forum. If they play 14th Street, they'll have to pay for their own advertising and there's no money, and besides, Rufus says, he's tired of playing *Paradise* before kids who just come to jump up and down and freak-out.

Steve Israel jumps into the wrangling on Julian's side, and tries to put Rufus down with some convoluted rap about some Black Panthers he says he met in Washington, D. C. during the young people's demonstration at the Presidential Inauguration; these Panthers were very friendly, very groovy guys who were much hipper than Rufus about where this country is at. A vehement exchange follows between Rufus and Steve, while those in the room listen quietly until it all winds up right where it had started: with Steve's assertion, and the unquestioning agreement of most of the others, that it's more important to play on 14th Street than on Broadway.

Rufus disagrees, calling it masturbatory. Somewhat more composed now, he shifts the argument back to Julian, and it goes on, eventually becoming deadlocked in repetition. Nowhere. The few actors remaining in the room begin to straggle out. Nothing has really been resolved. It never really seems to be and most likely never will be, but the old dialectic has had another self-defeating rerun.

The company was tired and would be even more exhausted by the time it reached New York; *Paradise,* though enshrined by a vast hippie following, was clearly not what it was intended to be; a "professional" audience would be demanding. Yet in Ann Arbor, Julian had told a rapt audience of students, "We should not stop speaking to the bourgeoisie who are willing to pay five and ten dollars to get to see the Living Theatre. . . . We cannot stop trying to communicate with this segment, for the revolution depends on reaching everyone and trying to effect change on all levels."

One wondered if Julian's heated polemics this afternoon had not been a cop-out rather than an aversion to selling out.

147

The Country in Winter

It is probably different from what the See America First billboards have in mind. Nevertheless, its immensity and its topography are not altered with the seasons; from one equinox to the next, it remains a big fucking country. To belabor the point to its fullest it is necessary to drive from its East Coast to the Pacific, the way it was settled. In following the westward trend of the early settlers one can see the gradual dissolution of the quasi-English temperament of the Eastern seaboard into the stagnant inland culture of the Midwest, and finally, the first signs of a pure American character in the Plains states. It is possible that the only true American culture exists today between Denver and the West Coast.

In winter. Endless. Endless hours on endless highways that cut through endless mountains or endless nothing. Perhaps the same is true in the summer months, but in winter the foliage, the grass, the wildlife . . . the "decorations" . . . are gone and all that remains is the terrain and climate: the bare essentials of nature. Sunless, rainless, flatness, dryness, highness, dampness, wetness, bleakness; there is always a feeling of lessness-ness. Weather loses all atmospheric meaning and materializes in bizarre quantitative forms—too much weather in Nebraska, none at all in Kansas City—and qualitative styles; weather in Chicago is very fast. Thirty miles-per-hour through a blinding blizzard in New York State, frozen windshield wipers. In the Donner Pass, winds that cause the car to skid out on icy roads, and the signs of engineering apology: Slippery when Wet or Frosty, Watch for Falling Rocks, Slide Area. Weather paranoia develops; America is full of weather.

Kansas City had no weather at all, just a gray, hanging *condition* that couldn't even work itself up to a decent drizzle. Neither cold nor mild, not even a noticeable temperature to stir the senses into a mood, and yet the streets are lined up with jagged banks of dirty snow so solidly packed that one has no idea of how long it has been there. So there must have been weather here at least once, but it must have come from someplace else—Nebraska, probably. It was as if they had tried weather once in Kansas City, but they hadn't liked it.

Beyond the industrialized, densely populated Northeast there is a Never-Never Again Land in which distance becomes irrelevant, mileage becomes meaningless; and as the mind sets up games to play to pass the time, there is the take-over of the *geographic imposition* and a reversal of the time-space continuum: it is not a question of miles-per-hour but a definite matter of hours-per-mile.

About two hours outside of Kansas City, heading west on Interstate 70, we are completely immersed in a dense, roiling atmospheric condition: heavy fog, sheets of rain, and a strong driving wind. It is easily recognizable as weather, and

150

in a funny way we were glad to run into it again. It lasted for the better part of an hour and gradually began to taper off. Up ahead the dark clouds break, giving way to a clear sky, and within the next hour it is over and we are driving through a landscape of deep blue sky and brilliant sunlight. The air is crisp and springlike. The earth, while retaining that territorial flatness that becomes aggressive simply by its sheer expanse, is now dark reddish brown and rich in color, although it's still winter-hard and impenetrable with now-and-then strips of unmelted snow. On either side for miles the land is strewn with small toylike drills, deceptively primitive looking mechanisms that pump oil from the ground with a cyclical precision that is almost surrealistic in its slow motion rhythm.

Hays, Kansas. A small herd of buffalo in a wire-fenced-in-field belonging to the university's agricultural school. We park by the road to take pictures of them, and, digging our mission, they move closer until they are just a few feet away on the other side of the fence. Poor scruffy creatures, they should be out on the Plains screwing like mad to avoid extinction. But here they are, the two huge males obligingly locking horns while a pair of young ones begin a clumsy game of tag. Others strike the old nickel pose; there's about fifty cents worth of buffalo in the flesh over there. The roll of film runs out, but before we can reload the camera, they stop and lumber off across the field. It's the classic buffalo act, but they've tightened it up since the documentaries.

February 3. Goodland, Kansas is on Route 70 about thirty miles from the Colorado border. It is not on the company's

151

itinerary—it's just a stop that Gianfranco and I make for gas and coffee. And having gassed and coffeed, we're leaving the gas station diner when a stocky, innocuous looking youngish man steps up and flashes a badge. He explains superfluously that he's a policeman and would like to see our identification. We hand over driver's licenses, passports, and car registration, and while he's sorting it all out, a patrol car pulls up and a cohort in full cop-drag gets out and walks over.

"Why are we being detained?" I ask.

"Routine check," says Innocuous, also cuing in Cop Drag that this is a speculative hassle that may or may not be worthwhile. Cop Drag nods and repeats the line. The sun glinting off his white helmet somehow puts it in italics even though it comes out "chack" in his delivery. They scrutinize our credentials with the kind of attention usually reserved for open brain surgery, Gianfranco's papers being in Italian posing the primary handicap. Or so it would seem to a relatively rational onlooker whose main concern is that the issue not be confused by the discovery of the full felony of marijuana in the luggage. Not to mention a misdemeanor's worth of hash in the glove compartment. We're traveling light, but Goodland, Kansas doesn't seem like the sort of place to make a test case of moderation.

"Which one of you is Ren-free?" one of them asks. It's not even the sort of place to be flat-chested. I tell them I am and leave them hanging with the Italian papers which they can't decipher. Being a strong believer in creative confusion, I add to the disorder a small inundation of press passes, most of which permit free access to New York City museums, but this is in smaller print; it's the large lettering that says PRESS that counts. These are passed between the two men without comment and then quickly tucked away in my passport, which the patrolman is holding.

"But you're from Italy," he addresses Gianfranco, more in accusation than observation. There's got to be something illegal about that.

"Why don't you just use my papers," I interrupt impatiently. "They're in English."

"But you weren't driving," snaps Innocuous, thus frustrating Cop Drag who seemed willing to negotiate this point for the sake of expediency. This is a purely intuitive assertion from Innocuous, because an enormous freight truck happened to have been refueling between our VW and the diner where he had stopped us; he couldn't possibly have seen who was at the wheel when we drove up. But having blurted out his gross assumption, correct though it was, he has now made it impossible to ignore the printed language barrier.

"We have to call Washington, D. C., and check this out," Cop Drag concludes, and having instructed us to wait in our car, the two of them get into the patrol car. Much static and bleeping, very impressive police things, and finally Innocuous alights and comes over to announce that the Chief of Police wants to see us. Follow the patrol car, no funny shit, and like that. And off we go.

Several minutes later we pull up at the police station and get out. They come over to escort us inside, and again I ask why we're being detained.

"Well, you're dressed something out of the ordinary for around here," replies Innocuous with a vague touch of

153

animosity in his tone. And he gets pissed off when I apologize for not looking like farmers.

Upstairs, the Chief of Police . . . F. E. (Fritz) Freeman, announces the nameplate on the desk. Our credentials are handed to him and, having motioned us into chairs facing his desk, he shuffles through them cautiously. As he does this, he asks us where we've been, where we're going, and similar questions that you wouldn't expect to be any of his business, but his manner is relaxed and courteous. He sets my papers aside, commenting only that I was "from the media" and goes through Gianfranco's things with more interest. Opening the leather binding that holds the driver's license, he scans it a moment and then turns and translates it, word for word, to our official escorts who are standing behind him. He relishes these moments of linguistic showmanship, and being so pointedly informed that everything is in order, the patrolman gets off an apologetic smile and his plainclothes accomplice looks sheepish. Bugging them further, the Chief explains that His Men aren't accustomed to dealing with foreign visitors such as ourselves. He shrewdly counters this put-down by saying that there has been trouble in the past with young people who look much the same as we do. We offer our sympathy. He goes on to say how extensively he, himself, has traveled in Europe, adding that he knows first-hand how often people there are stopped by the police and asked to show their identification papers. He doesn't elaborate on this point. He doesn't have to: he has been speaking to us in French.

Our papers are returned and the patrolman is instructed to escort us back to Route 70. Turning to leave his office,

154

THE COUNTRY IN WINTER

we are confronted by a small crowd huddled in the hallway outside of the door. People have left their offices and come to gape at us. The wheels of the Law are not being turned; Order has taken a recess to get a whiff of the Strange. How many freaks and Mad Bombers; Visitors From Another Planet and Commie fags; hippies, Yippies, and Siamese axe murderers joined at the base of the spine have stopped for gas and coffee in Goodland, Kansas, within that short span of time? Unapprehended, speeding on down Route 70 without undue process of law. How many of them have we run interference for?

The crowd parts for us to follow the grinning patrolman down the stairs, and half way down we look back and see (Fritz) standing on the landing.

"Bonne chance," he calls with a jaunty salute. (Fritz) is a smooth mother.

YOU ARE LEAVING KANSAS. COME BACK SOON. Fuck you. WELCOME TO COLORADO. Are you sure?

But for a long time it looks just like Kansas. The hours-per-mile syndrome returns for a while, only to be interrupted by a gray mountain mass that juts up on the distant horizon. The interruption is temporary, and the jagged mass gradually recedes in the rear-view mirror, leaving us once again in the unbroken flatness. The road begins to climb, slowly at first, in gentle preparation for the sharp ascent it will take to reach the Boulder-Denver plateau, and suddenly the Rockies are running along to the left, soon barricading the horizon ahead, ice-peaked and frozen against the cloudless sky. Their encirclement is protective until it is realized that the

155

only way pass them is *over* them. But later for vertigo and acrophobia; there is a promise in the moment: Colorado will be different. Colorado is more than different—it is grand and beautiful; Colorado was a surge of energy, a refueling of a spirit dragged and dampened through the Midwest and the Plains.

Five days of freak February weather between Denver and Boulder, mountain sun and temperatures in the mid-sixties. But by the third day the old bronchial thing has entrenched itself, reminding me, as it first did in Spain, that I cannot survive in comfort in a healthy climate where the altitude is beyond the reach of air pollution. Rufus, hacking and wheezing from what is said to be pleurisy, consoles through a fistful of soggy kleenex: "There is absolutely no reason why we should be expected to live a mile above sea level."

A day's excursion to Rocky Mountain National Park gives a preview of what's to come. The signs of change: Winding Road, Watch For Falling Rocks, Reduce Speed: 20 MPH. HILL: one of the great understatements of traffic control in the west. The unnerving squiggles on diamond-shaped signs; roads that defy verbal description, reducing traffic bureaus to idiotic symbols, maniacally yellow rhombi capriciously imbedded in the shoulder of the road. The "shoulder of the road": a narrow space that separates you from a ravine that happens to be at sea level.

The short span of straightaway that suddenly becomes a Winding Road, at its summit the View Zap from the dangling precipice, the tortuous descent; the repetitious rerun of the terror and the thrill broken only by the diversion of

156

your entire life racing before your eyes; the magnificent pageantry of topographical horror. God, please spare me from another fucking view. And that night you worry about those pains in your head.

Wyoming. Cheyenne. Laramie. Names enhanced by legend and the Western. Do the men look like Randolph Scott? The highway cuts across the lowest point of the Rockies, a frozen, massive sky-desert secured to this planet only by this wide band of concrete . . . scoured by the brutal wind that soars through the altitudinous depression created by its good intentions. Late afternoon. Driving directly into a blazing sun that throws dense purple shadows across the harsh land. It is a silent, haunted world that belongs to the dead who tried to settle it, to the ghosts of those who were only passing through.

The Great Salt Lake, the desert and the salt flats. There is a feeling of oppression in the emptiness. A night passed in Elko, Nevada; the casino, topless go-go dancers and a twangy Country Western trio behind the bar. Twangy: the only word that could appropriately describe the sound of a Country Western trio. A sea of cowboy hats in front of the bar. Roulette, craps, the jackpot. A ferocious woman playing an entire row of nickel machines shrieks at us when we stop for a second look at her, "THESE ARE *MY* MACHINES!!"

A narrow highway stretches across a desert that has no weather at all; on either edge of this barren world, mountains, one-dimensional and black beneath their sparse veil of snow . . . today we are racing through a gigantic lithograph . . . until the road turns southward and aims toward Reno; en route the overcast breaks into blue sky and earth colors appear, greens and browns, a limited but welcome spectrum that inexplicably arouses a desperate urge to get to an ocean.

Introduction to California: a blinding rainstorm that makes the Donner Pass almost impassable, ten feet of snow forming a solid wall on either side; the Ice Corridor to the Pacific. On the western slope the turbulence vanishes completely, giving way to rich earth and thick foliage; clear air that promises either mountain or sea. Either one could have been hallucinated, so sharp and immediate is the change. And though I have never been here before, a strange sense of *déjà-vu*. It is the feedback of Hitchcock movies.

Northern California and Oregon. It is either raining or threatening to rain. The treacherous coast highway tunneling for hundreds of miles through towering redwood forests: another damned natural phenomenon. When nature is so overpowering, silence is induced, for any conversation would be banal. The mind-games have been played out long ago, the last one, replayed because of cheating, slipping away over yesterday's desert. Silence . . . the engine's steady drone through the mindscape where reason is being absurded into infinite convolutions that always connect back to the loose string of reason. As usual, I have been excessive and improvident: I have left no thoughts for today.

Mental geography: flat, barren, badly in need of irrigation and fertilization.

Mother Nature's unequal distribution of her assets: for two days we get the Tree Zap, and rain, lots of rain. Some

158

**Welcome to Berkeley,
the Theatre is in
the street**

WANTED, Eldridge Cleaver (*lower right-hand corner*); motel lobby, Holbrook, Arizona

The Mat Piece; Rite of Opposite Forces, Rung VI

The Rite of Universal Intercourse, Rung IV

The Liberated Audience / The Tree of Life

◀ The Mat Piece; Straight Theatre, San Francisco

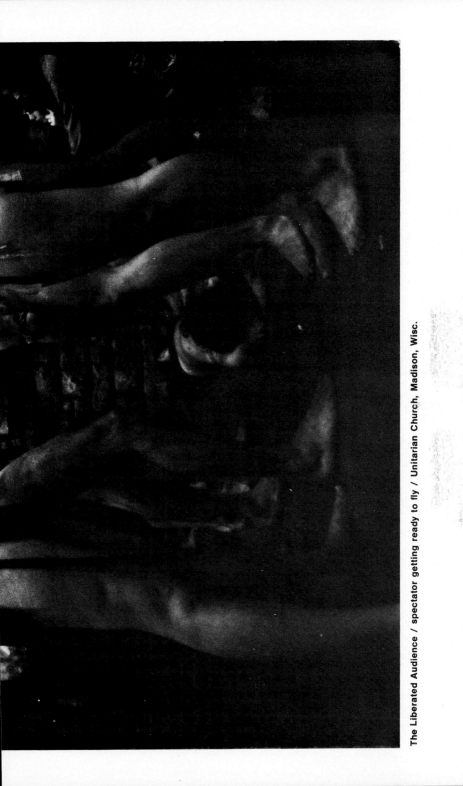

The Liberated Audience / spectator getting ready to fly / Unitarian Church, Madison, Wisc.

Julian in interview on Hippie Hill, Golden Gate Park, San Francisco

say it has been raining for weeks, maybe months by now, in California. Every night we collapse into a motel and turn on the tube, and somebody always has a word or two to say about mudslides and flash floods and property loss and deaths and student riots at the universities—to be followed by earthquakes. The eastern seaboard is buried in blizzards. Santa Barbara is being inundated by off-shore grease, and somewhere along the way Nixon was inaugurated. Is it any wonder I have nothing to think about today?

Late in the afternoon I have two thoughts in a row: With all that tissue paper and cardboard that enshrouds everything we buy, how is it possible to spend two whole days snaking through this stifling vegetation? Damned if I know. And how can these vast tracts of land lie wasted and empty when the world is supposedly overpopulated and underfed? God knows. Does He?

What the hell am I doing here? Speeding, says the cop, and crossing a double line on a curve.

LEAVING CALIFORNIA. WELCOME TO OREGON. Surely they can't mean that, can they?

Five days driving from Boulder to Portland. It could've been done in two or three. What difference does it make when it could also have been done by plane in a couple of hours? To drive it in five days is to experience the most majestic boredom imaginable.

California

Who Do I Have To Fuck To Get Off This Tour?—because it was here that a Displacement of Disaster principle came into play. Before one upheaval could be absorbed and resolved, another one set in, making it almost impossible to keep them separate, the conclusion of one tending to precipitate the next crisis. When departmentalization collapsed, Tony the bus driver was the only accurate source of basic information—Is there a show tonight? Where's the theatre? Where's the hotel? The party? Is the tour over? Can we go now?

February 18–20: Berkeley

Perhaps a scorecard would be a more appropriate device for projecting the circumstances. But that would imply that a competition of equal merit had existed, and such was hardly the case. The Living Theatre was unprepared from the start and by the end it had suffered an ignoble defeat.

Little money had been available for advance publicity.

161

What Mark Amitin had been able to borrow from private sources had been stretched as far as possible, and there had been a certain amount of goodwill from the local underground press. In retrospective consideration, it's doubtful that an adequate budget would have affected the situation and created a better climate for the Living. The Berkeley campus was in the midst of demonstrations that had been going on for a month with an acceleration of police-inflicted violence. University of Chicago, University of Wisconsin at Madison, Reed College—across the country students were confronting school administrations and being answered by police, and here in California both Berkeley and nearby San Francisco State Teachers College were in turmoil. Added to the fuel revolt was Assemblyman and member of the State Board of Regents John Stull's call for the ouster of Herbert Marcuse from the faculty of the University of California at San Diego on the grounds that Marcuse was a revolutionary who was stirring the students' unrest. At universities across California, students were massing in protest of the threatened dismissal of Marcuse. Nothing done for the Living Theatre would have altered this reality in any way: something done *by* them might have, at least in Berkeley where they had arrived for three performances at the three-thousand-seat Berkeley Community Theatre. On the first night an audience of 350 came out to see *Mysteries;* the second night *Frankenstein* had its smallest audience, 600; *Paradise* was the third night. . . .

But the afternoon of that third day, an afternoon on the riot-torn Berkeley campus, had marked the turning point, and the night in the theatre had brought on an acute re-

162

evaluation, a confirmation on my part that certain reservations . . . reservations having nothing to do with the artistic
work of the Living Theatre . . . were unfortunately justified.
These reservations stemmed in part from having observed
too many contradictions between the company's ideological
pronouncements and their practical manifestations, but I
had tactfully attributed these inconsistencies and the facile
rationales they inspired to the commercial structure of the
American tour, which was not conducive to unconditional
anarchy, and I had made allowances for it, as one is taught
to ignore sloppiness when one is a guest in a house. On a
deeper level of private consciousness, as a Quaker, I had in
recent years begun to question the tenets of passive resistance
as an effective instrument in an increasingly violent reality
that kills and maims and sorts its casualties according to
Style. The Kennedys had been heroes, and therefore worthy
of monuments, while martyrs were useful as symbols; Gandhi
was killed and King had been shot. But the fact remained
that they were all dead. There was no end in sight for the
cycle of violence . . . and some said that it no longer mat-
tered, since due to mismanagement of the planet, time was
running out anyway . . . and yet retaliatory action against
a violent provocation seemed to me a biological reflex when
the instinct for survival was threatened. Berkeley did not
resolve the moral quandary; it did give a personal perspective that had not been available, nor even particularly necessary, before, and I understood that passive resistance was
dangerous and unnatural. . . .
Before the tear gas and the pepper fog congested the
air, when the clubs still dangled beneath policemen's jackets

and bulged beneath their yellow raincoats, I had stood with the students, perhaps a thousand of them, in Sproul Plaza this bright sunny mid-morning, and, admittedly having but superficial insight into what was at stake, possessed only by the brazen *involvement on moral principle,* I had watched the confusion of policemen trying to "contain" a nonviolent demonstration. Alameda County Sheriff's Deputies; California Highway Patrolmen; the Oakland police, seasoned in terrorism by Hell's Angels and Black Panthers; and the Berkeley police, unable to go it alone in this hot-bed of pacifistic revolt—dozens of them with yellow slickers, gleaming white helmets, billy-clubs and walkie-talkies: packaged for trouble and facing the "enemy," the Third World Liberation Front, the striking faculty and teachers union, and hundreds of students, all of them, with varying motivations and objectives, demanding what boiled down to *a relevant* education. This day held a special promise of an escalation of the violence that had ripped the campus on other days like today, when the elements are friendly and brutality is made comfortable.

Before the gas masks and science-fiction machines came out, when the walkie-talkies still bleeped directives for bizarre and meaningless maneuvers, I had stood amidst the tension, watching the policemen and wondering why the old ones barked and growled and why the young ones looked old and averted their eyes when I stared at them. And as they stood in absurd formation on the crest of the embankment, I had dug that they looked like mechanical toys, like prizes in a macabre carnival concession. And I had wondered what they were doing on that campus in a situation

164

that didn't concern them. And yes, it did occur to me that the same question could be put to me: neither instructor nor student, and curiousity being the only appreciable consequence of my own education. With No Business Being There the expedient epitaph for the testy stone-cutter who keeps the records straight, conscience was my only alibi.

Before the tensions exploded and frustration caused the first tear gas grenade to be tossed into the crowd—the inevitable point at which an observer becomes a participant; before the pepper fog scorched our faces and made us cry like children—the point from which commitment can be measured; when the police were merely nervous and the mob was simply alert, I had crazily anticipated, no, hoped for, something—the materialization of the Living *en masse*.

They had kept abreast of what was happening here; for the past month they had been reading and talking about these demonstrations and following them on television, and now they were just a few minutes' walk to the campus from the hotel. Surely some of them must have sense enough to round up the others and get up here to support the students. The police had managed to clear the demonstrators from the center of the Plaza, barricading them around its periphery; the Living would just have to pass the cordon and walk into the emptied space in their funny costumes, a "Chord" would ease the tensions. Given their unpublicized circumstances, it seemed a simple matter of public relations that could win a few friends and influence some serious people for a change. But it was a fantasy that never materialized. Too spaced, too lazy, too fucked up on drugs, they never showed up to try to prevent the three o'clock riot.

165

When all the tear gas canisters had been volleyed back and forth until they had fallen and exploded, when people had been clubbed and arrested for resisting arrest by dutiful officers . . . when all that remains is the blood and the tears, there is little patience with the pious dialectic of "anarchism" and "revolution" that refuse to heed the illustrated reality: nonviolence is a one-way pact; the police have yet to sit in on its negotiations.

Gassed and beaten in that afternoon's confrontation, a Berkeley audience filled the theatre that night, and when *Paradise* ended, it had been transformed into a full-blown fiasco for the Living Theatre. An hour or so before the show actually started, a "rehearsal" was taking place in the dressing room, and based as it was on a recap of news reports and the evening telecast, it gave off a faint whiff of disaster that grew heavier as it progressed. There was a small covey of actors claiming to have "witnessed" the riot, and they offered first-hand information concerning the prevalence of tear gas in the air and people running by as they emerged from a shopping tour of hippie boutiques and head shops along Telegraph Avenue; since such shopping expeditions weren't unusual, this information was only enlightening because it was accepted by many who had not ventured even that far from the hotel. It should be noted that three actors from the company were known to have taken part in the actual melee on the campus, and tonight one of them had refused to go on in *Paradise*, a boycott that was maintained for the remainder of the tour; he has since left the company.

Incensed by this rehearsal, by the sheer negligence and

fraudulence that riddled it, playing *Paradise* tonight appeared as hypocritical as playing Broadway, according to Julian's convictions, would have been. My disappointment over the Living's failure to appear on the Berkeley campus to try to deter the violence of the afternoon, could be passed off as an overestimation of either their dedication or their ability to deal with such a situation outside of the theatre; but now it was more discouraging when no alternative could be found for the evident conclusion that they were full of shit.

It did not take long for the audience to arrive at the same unfortunate conclusion. Students, faculty, residents of Berkeley, they were all ahead of the Living, and if *Paradise* had lacked relevance on numerous other occasions, it would be thoroughly embarrassing at Berkeley . . . and later on in San Francisco where the Hashbury community had not wanted to see it, not even for free; they wanted to see *Frankenstein* or *Antigone*. The tour had been much too long; the Midwestern stretch had exhausted the company but left them complacent and smugly enshrined as the hippest expedition since Lewis and Clark. Unprepared for Berkeley, it is apparent tonight that they were only hip by default. Unable, unwilling, to grasp this approximation of a functioning paradise, the world they presumed to envision was reduced to embarrassing harangues and meaningless slogans.

"I'm not allowed to smoke marijuana" . . . a joke when it is sold and smoked on the streets; *"I'm not allowed to travel without a passport"* . . . this is not the young audience's idea of a trip; *"You can't live if you don't have money"* . . .

167

this one conclusively disproven when the Living arrived penniless in San Francisco ten days later. There was something wrong with the opening "Rite" and it was not long before things got worse . . . *"Be the students at Columbia!"* a line in the script an actor shouts; sometimes in the more agreeable past it had gotten applause. In Berkeley the audience had responded with a resounding round of "Bullshit! Bullshit!" That was clearly a critical assessment of where *Paradise* was at tonight. Due either to the actor's ignorance or to Julian's stubborn refusal to adjust the performance to the situation, either one a perfectly plausible excuse for the insult, this line was tossed out in Berkeley where revolt has been a reality for at least four years.

Pandemonium, angry students shouting demands that the box office proceeds be turned over to the bail fund . . . and in the lobby a group of ten middle-aged adults, probably tagged "bohemians" before the "beats" and "hippies" came into the vocabulary, are demanding refunds from the road manager and the actor who had refused to play. "We have been giving money to the students' bail fund . . . this is a farce," a man declares. Another insists there was better "theatre" that afternoon on Telegraph Avenue; if the company needs money, go up there and ask for donations, but don't ask for four dollars a seat for this. . . . A lady lawyer is commenting that New York must be "very provincial" to have swallowed this. They are echoing the sentiments being vehemently expressed inside the theatre. Pointing to Julian who stands in the midst of the chaos on stage, the actor says, "He's the 'manager.' Go up and tell him how you feel."

168

"No," says the lady. "That's just what he wants us to do, and we're not interested in that game." The group leaves.

At twelve-thirty, having been dragged only as far as its Fifth Rung, *Paradise* is finally brought to a halt, not as an act of mercy, but because it is brought to Julian's attention that the contract that Mark Amitin had signed with the theatre management stipulates that the theatre be closed at midnight. There was some protest from a few of the Living, but it seemed purely perfunctory and wasn't supported by what remained of the spectators. When it was over and the company had returned to the hotel, there was no indication that they understood how tremendous and significant a fiasco the performance had been. The main concern appeared to be getting to a party at a hippie commune in the Berkeley hills.

Depending on one's point of view, it is either interesting or superfluous to note that this was the first performance of *Paradise Now* that had attracted no attention from the local authorities: the Living Theatre was not considered a danger by Berkeley standards.

Coinciding with the eviction from the theatre, notice came that there was an unpaid tax bill that amounted to $25,000: the Internal Revenue Service was seizing all future box office receipts.

Revenue agents had arrived at the theatre too late to impound tonight's receipts, a coincidence in itself, since Mark had been going over them in the box office while the show was in progress. Counting the proceeds and going over

169

the ledgers, he had worked undisturbed in the quiet office away from the bedlam, when suddenly he was distracted by an unexplicable uneasiness, a "funny feeling," that had grown more persistent and disquieting. Finally he had put everything into his briefcase and walked back to his hotel where he continued the accounting while the agents were back at the theatre.

The next morning, Friday, February 21. It is learned that all of the Living Theatre bank accounts in the state of California have been frozen. Opened in Berkeley, Los Angeles, and San Francisco for the advance ticket sales, with the exception of the former, these accounts were said to be fairly sizable, at least enough to encourage the continuation of the tour. There was a terrible irony to this current crisis; hoping to show that he was trustworthy and honest, Mark Amitin had opened these accounts in the name of the Living Theatre. Neither he nor Bob Cohen had been informed by the Radical Theatre Repertory that this was never to be done, that nothing was to be put in the Living Theatre's name, and as it now turned out, these temporary accounts had existed in that name in several other cities on the tour. It was also disclosed that temporary box office personnel had been bonded in the name of the Living Theatre, because Gottlieb was said to have advised Bob Cohen that no bonding agency would insure an organization with the word "radical" in its name. Theoretically the government seizures could have started as early as Boston; why they didn't is as open to conjecture as what happened to the $7,000 Gottlieb claimed to have paid in payroll taxes back in mid-January when the company wasn't paid in Madison, Wisconsin. Having been given power-of-attorney by the RTR in order to sign contracts and handle the accounts, Cohen and Amitin were also subject to possible indictment and imprisonment along with Gottlieb, who had apparently withheld important information while certainly knowing about these bank accounts and employee bonds. There also existed now the possibility of the *Frankenstein* set being impounded as had happened to *The Brig* set in 1964.[1]

The Berkeley engagement having been the disappointment that it was, there is only enough money to pay the hotel bill and give the actors ten dollars apiece to tide them over until a decision is reached. Should they collect the Equity bond and go back to Europe now? Or should they continue on in the hope of finding some solution in Los Angeles? Calls are made. The dean at the University of Southern California in LA promises Julian a check for an advance of $3,000 on Monday morning. On Saturday afternoon we decamp from Berkeley.

But those on the Big Bus have persuaded Tony to take the scenic coast highway, and half-way to LA he is forced to turn back because of mudslides and floods—the road has been washed out by the month-long rainstorms. That night, without food or money, yesterday's ten dollars long gone, the company sleeps in a church in Carmel. They arrive in LA late Sunday night.

---

[1] *The Brig* set had later been placed on sale at government auction. It had been bought back by Julian for the reported sum of eleven dollars.

171

February 24–28: Los Angeles

Los Angeles isn't the sort of city that inspires affection. In the rain it's as dank and depressing as a seaside resort would be under the same conditions, and in brilliant sunlight it sprawls in a state of unequivocal tackiness. To drive through LA is to see the Many Faces of Queens dotted with palm trees that jut like flimsy feather dusters, pocked by incidental vegetation that appears artificial, "posed"; it may be the only place on earth where nature looks ridiculous. A plastic environment lacking the substance of a solid synthetic, styrofoam is its true medium.

LA is Wheel City. According to the 1968 World Almanac, there are over three million registered automobiles in its metropolitan area, a statistic that breaks down into the highest ratio of car-per-person of any major city in the world: one car for every 2.2 citizens . . . the two-tenths residents presumably being those who have already achieved an advanced stage of bio-technological development in which the only part of the body that exists at birth is that portion extending from the top of the head to the bottom ledge of a car window. Having become nothing more than a vestigial appendage, the rest of the body has disappeared, absorbed into the automobile, its genitalia incorporated into the design, its metabolism a matter of revolutions-per-minute. These are the Car People, death-defying mutants who live on the Freeways and strike terror in the hearts of all who venture into their territory. A further touch of endearment comes from the number of freaks on the tube and in the streets who are predicting an earthquake, a prognosis that appears belated; one suspects that there's been an earthquake, but no one has noticed it. A couple of nights after our arrival a "small earthquake" is reported to have occurred in downtown LA; it is said to have taken place simultaneously with another one farther north on the San Andreas Fault. It must have been beneficial because the next day the sun came out.

It would be difficult to like LA under the best of circumstances, and the Living are here under the worst. By now it has been determined that the government seizures are based on the old tax bill, an amount in the area of $25,000, which dates back to 1964 when the Living Theatre left the country. From the beginning of the negotiations for this return tour, it had been assumed by the producers that some settlement would have to be reached with the federal government on the back-tax issue if the company was to be allowed reentry into the United States. To go back before its return in September of 1968, Attorney Jerald Ordover, one of the legal representatives retained for the Living Theatre, had offered the government a settlement on the basis that the old corporation, Living Theatre Productions, Incorporated, was defunct but that the Becks were willing to assume a certain amount of the liability. A percentage based on this liability was offered, but the government, feeling that the tour would make a lot more money than the sum proposed, had rejected the settlement. Thus it happened that when the Becks and company entered the country in September, no formal arrangement had been made for the payment of the old tax bill; consequently the tour had been set up as explained earlier, and it was thought to be understood by all concerned with keeping it afloat that as long as no bank accounts existed in the name of the Living Theatre, and

173

as long as the payroll taxes were paid this time around, the chances of complications with the Internal Revenue Service and government seizure would be minimal.

In point of fact, the federal government had been trying to get advance information on the itinerary of the tour, but it had been unsuccessful. Apparently guessing that it would eventually reach California, the IRS's Oakland office had been alerted, and the mission became elementary when a series of bank accounts actually turned up in the company's name. The government had ordered the accounts to be impounded, and now, in LA, there is a feeble hint of rescue when it is learned that the legality of these seizures is being brought under question in Washington, D. C., where Attorney Ordover is meeting with federal representatives. Eventually the government does concede that the seizures are, in effect, illegal, based as they are on the old tax bill. These monies cannot go to pay a tax debt that is the responsibility of the Becks, not of the present company which is incorporated as the Living Theatre of Europe, a cooperative organization owned by all of its members who, theoretically speaking, are employees in America of the Radical Theatre Repertory. However—the feeble hope of financial salvation fades—these monies must be attached to the *new* payroll tax debt, a matter of something between ten and twelve thousand dollars, which seems to have been neglected.

It's a raw, rainy night when the Big Bus deposits its cargo of weary actors and children at the Starlite Motel, a dreary place whose squalor provides a fitting environment for the

174

dismal circumstances. Having gotten to LA two days before the company, Mark had caught sight of the motel's neon marquee from a freeway . . . DOUBLES $11 . . . and with economy uppermost in mind, he had stopped in and reserved rooms for everyone. Atoning for this somewhat, he had also managed to borrow $400 from producer Michael Butler, who had insured repayment of his loan by agreeing to cash the $3,000 check from the University of Southern California, and each of the Living gets a ten-dollar share of the loan on arrival and goes off to take care of the most immediate problem: starvation.

As in Berkeley, the question again is whether to go back to New York after this engagement, which would mean that the impounded advance sale in San Francisco would have to be returned to the ticket-holders; or, on the other hand, to go on to San Francisco and play there on the chance that the seizures were illegal and that the monies would be returned to the company. At this point it's known only that the government action *might* be illegal; as yet news of the new debt has not been transmitted out to the Coast. The night passes slowly with no sign of the Becks until quite late. They finally arrive and settle in, after which they are joined by a few others who want to discuss the issues. A curious attitude is said to have been expressed at this small gathering by a couple of people who appeared to be unexpectedly impatient and irritated with those who didn't seem to be able to comprehend the *value* of what was happening: if the tour is forced to a premature end because of nonpayment of taxes, the Living Theatre has once again been victimized by the American government and forced

175

into exile. Such publicity would be useful in Europe when they returned, the speculation is said to have gone.

It could have worked had they not already been victimized by the RTR. The reality was that they were stranded, and it was virtually impossible to find a sympathetic "angel" who was willing to bail them out. The only solution was for them to keep working for whatever money could be circumvented from government seizure until they got back to New York.

It isn't necessary, or particularly interesting, for that matter, to give a detailed recount of the incident that took place on the second night when we returned to the Starlite Motel after the show. A minor disaster that segues into the next crisis, this nasty little affair was provoked by the manager who had placed a table across the main entrance in an attempt to keep us out until we agreed to his equally shaky demand for a week's rent in advance. Despite the management's immediate retaliation with physical intervention . . . to call it violence would dignify their clumsy efforts . . . when the rickety obstacle was casually shoved aside, the skirmish was brief, probably because none of the Living stood still long enough for a blow to make contact. Once inside the lobby the commotion was accelerated when one of the baby-sitters came down to inform us that our rooms had been searched and our luggage ransacked by the proprietor and his cohorts; concealed by the shadows, she had silently followed them as they went from room to room along the concrete ramp that encircled the building's exterior and gave access to all the rooms. In no way trying to interfere with the search, her intent was to witness it and try to make sure

176

nothing was stolen. However, it soon developed that a third party was involved in going through our rooms, and a tape recorder belonging to one of the actors had been stolen. Funnily enough, this demand for payment happened to coincide with the dispersal of the $3,000 among the Living, so it was really a matter of their being unwilling . . . and rightly so . . . to agree to the unreasonable request for advance payment and resenting the uncalled-for treatment to which they were being subjected for no rational reason. The manager's reasons for instigating this incident were as obscure as his reasons for subsequently calling the police, but nevertheless, four officers arrived amidst a confusion of infuriated Living and entourage, a steel band from Trinidad which was also lodged here, and a small contingent of Black Panthers that had suddenly materialized. Actually this represented the high point in the lobby culture over the past two days and gave it a certain esprit that was definitely lacking in its motley assortment of "regulars"—biscuit-faced B-movie rejects, muscle fags whose teeth seemed to have been capped by piano-tuners, starlets-cum-hooker—flitting in and out of the elevator, scurrying along the rain-swept ramp, coming to light in the lobby, which took on the appearance of a perpetual out-take. This was the first time we had stayed at a hotel and given it *class*.

Possibly because they were outnumbered by such a distinguished collection of freaks, the Starlite staff agreed to settle for payment for the two nights we had stayed there, for what they were entitled to, that is to say. And possibly because they had possibly been greased by the manager, who had called one of them into his office "to explain the

177

situation," the police officers just hung around, doing nothing one way or another. Our registration cards are "lost," rates higher than those printed on the cards or on the marquee outside are demanded; at the clamorous persistence of Julian and others the cards are "found" and checked against our receipts; we have been overcharged. What should we do? we ask the officers. That's a "civil case," they smile. Get a lawyer. The stolen tape recorder makes a miraculous reappearance, "found" by one of the hotel employees, and one of its speakers is still missing. Shrugging and smiling, the officers watch it all, and when all the bills have been overpaid they depart, having admonished us to watch our language in the future. It's obscene.

The next morning, without noticeable regret, we move to the Hotel Figueroa in downtown LA, luxury compared to the Starlite Zone, and the rates are the same. But by week's end hotel bills won't matter. We can't pay them anyway.

Bus bills, taxes, frozen accounts, money for food—the crises continue, while a rumor makes the rounds that the RTR has declared bankruptcy and dissolved itself. This is quickly followed by a second rumor that holds the first to be untrue; only the telephones at the RTR have been removed due to nonpayment of bills totalling over a thousand dollars. Meanwhile the shows are going on at the University of Southern California and monies are successfully diverted from bank accounts. The only problem seems to be mounting pressure from the door to prevent performances of *Paradise,* the first one scheduled for Friday night, followed by *Mysteries* on

Saturday night, and then a second *Paradise* closing the engagement on Sunday night, the second of March. The first night of *Paradise* rolls around bringing complications before it even begins.

Friday, 8:30 P.M. The company mills around on stage in the empty theatre of the Bovard Auditorium, while two very nervous young men, leaders of a student activities committee responsible for inviting the Living Theatre to USC, take turns trying to reach the dean from a phone in the wings. Bob Cohen hurtles back and forth like a frenzied yo-yo between Julian, standing on stage with an air of serenity that suggests the phantom string propelling Cohen, and the two distressed fellows on the phone, who try to absorb Cohen's frenetic impact before it comes round again. It is said that earlier in the week the dean, fully aware of their desperate financial straits, made a verbal agreement to pay the company what was due them through tonight's performance. But the dean has not as yet been tracked down, and everyone awaits word from him, or more specifically, money from him, which was supposedly promised before this performance. And a strike is mentioned in the event that it is not forthcoming.

Meanwhile, from beyond the barred doors to the lobby, a mob of students is shrieking and pounding and making a clamorous threat of reprisal if things are delayed much longer. Cohen is dispatched to the lobby to explain what's happening inside, why the show may not go on, and the deafening din subsides to a sympathetic roar of temporary appeasement.

The dean is finally located by phone and he seems to

179

have undergone a rather severe alteration in his former thinking, contending now that the printed contractual agreement calls for payment on the night of the final performance —something that everyone had probably known out front; what would have been the point of the verbal agreement otherwise? And having reneged on this verbal amendent, he has now placed the Living in a position of either continuing to perform without being able to feed themselves, or else breaking the written contract by refusing to go on. A decision is made to fulfill the contractual commitment and do the shows. That settled, a fire marshal comes forth to lay down a few stringent regulations as to the number of people permitted on stage. Ignoring the fact that on previous nights the stage had supported the three-ton *Frankenstein* set, he chooses to insist that it may collapse if more than fifty people stand on it tonight. He appoints Julian personally responsible for any smoking in the theatre, in the dressing rooms, in the world for that matter. It's an unusually heavy hassle, and he withdraws from the center of attention only to be replaced by a police official whose "opener" is that there are "five thousand" cops surrounding the building—a euphemism for Don't Fuck Around, but a bit of an exaggeration. The simple reality of the situation is that there are thirty-or-so helmeted cops clutching gas masks and standing in rigid formation right outside of the stage entrance as a motorcade of eight unmarked cars, four fuzz apiece, is parked with engines humming in the driveway just ahead of them.

Inside the theatre *Paradise* is careening along on a level of amiable bedlam that it hasn't attained since Boulder,

180

and in the darkened auditorium I approach the fire marshal and hold out my PRESS pass to the Museum of Modern Art. Seeing only the big print, he immediately tells me that he can't talk to me, can't give me "an official statement": "I was just told to come here by the dean," he says. And plain-clothesmen with walkie-talkies roam the aisles, reporting God-knows-what from amidst a screaming horde whose revelry seems to be generated by the unrest of the author-ities.

In the smoke-filled dressing room a few people sit around and talk about what's happening outside the theatre.

"Have they put on their yellow raincoats yet?" asks Mel Clay.

No.

"You're new to the revolution, baby. Don't worry about the fuzz 'til they put on the yellow raincoats. That's when they mean business. The rest is all bullshit."

The yellow raincoats never came out, and everyone went home after the show. He was right.

The following day notice is given that the last two shows, *Mysteries* and *Paradise,* have been canceled. This is a situa-tion quite similar to the one at MIT, except that this time the dean is refusing to pay for the canceled shows, which had been sold out. Under the contract, reparations were required, since the company, despite the threatened strike when the verbal agreement was breached, had in no way broken the printed agreement.

That weekend Attorney Ordover flew out from New York, and Monday morning he, Julian, Cohen, and Carl Einhorn

181

met with administration officials in an effort to reach a settle-ment. Beginning early Monday morning, this meeting was to consume most of the afternoon. Meanwhile the rest of the company checked out of their rooms to avoid being charged for an extra day and awaited marching orders in the lobby and around the pool of the hotel. Friendly and sympathetic to the plight of the homeless Living, the management took polite interest in it all, efficiently relaying phone calls and agreeing that the troupe should indeed be paid. However, in the event that it should not indeed be paid, they had taken the precaution of holding our luggage in an orderly collection in the center of the lobby where discreet sur-veillance could be maintained from the desk.

The urgent problems here were the hotel bill and then getting the company on the road for San Francisco where it was supposed to open the following night at the Nourse Auditorium. By 3:30 in the afternoon word came that the USC administration had agreed to pay enough money to cover the hotel expenses and feed the Living as far as San Francisco. That settled, Julian and Carl decided to leave the discussion and get the company to San Francisco, while Ordover, having succeeded in getting the administration to concede that it had no cause to cancel the shows and no claim that the Living Theatre had breached its contract, was to remain in LA until the rest of the finances had been settled. In continuing to debate this issue, Ordover was con-cerned with two things: the money was needed for taxes, and it was needed to help get the troupe back to Europe. He stayed on for two more days, during which time USC agreed to pay $1,500 of the monies due, still not the entire balance owed, but it was wired to the company in San Francisco. University representatives claimed that it would take two more weeks before a full accounting could be completed (ticket-holders had to be reimbursed for the canceled shows, checks had to clear, and so forth) and the meetings ended in a tentative accord based upon an estimate of profits from the engagement. When the accounting was finally completed, a sum considerably less than what had been estimated was sent, at which point the Radical Theatre Repertory fired Ordover and hired another lawyer to try to press the case further.

But for the moment, the hotel bill is paid, a small food allowance is distributed, and luggage is loaded onto the waiting vehicles. It's 4:30 in the afternoon when the caravan finally heads north again for San Francisco.

March 4–19: San Francisco

The Nourse Auditorium is closed to the Living Theatre and the advance sale has been impounded from the theatre and from shops selling tickets in different areas as well. The News of The Day. Again, whether to stay or leave for New York. Hotels are out of the question, food being the basic issue here where the prospects of supporting themselves appears even bleaker than before. When the $1,500 comes from LA it is apportioned among the Living in allowances of five dollars a day.

Occupants of a Haight Street commune offer the use of their premises for our headquarters and make room for fifteen of the Living Theatre entourage, sixty-some adults and children in all, while the rest of us are welcomed into private homes by friendly, caring strangers . . . artists, students, business and professional people, hippies, the young and the older . . . free and sharing human beings who know only that we are here and in very bad shape.

In the late afternoon a man of medium height bustles through the Haight Street commune, his neatly trimmed dark hair and cheerfully animated face visible above the enormous bags of groceries clutched in his arms. Warm greetings are exchanged with the young people in the large comfortable rooms, as some girls join him as he moves on quickly, purposefully toward the kitchen in the rear of the house. The heavy parcels are deposited on a table, and as he stands now empty-handed and catching his breath for a second, one notices his black clerical garb and the sculpted metal cross suspended from his white-collared neck. He removes his jacket, rolls the black shirtsleeves above his elbows, puts on a protective striped denim apron. In motion again, quickly, efficiently darting about the sunlit kitchen, unpacking the groceries, sorting pots and pans, instructing those waiting to help him, he speaks gently, yet with a certain breathless quality that suggests someone whose thoughts are ahead of his words. He is the Right Reverend Michael Francis Itkin, formerly of New York, now shepherd of San Francisco's Free Church, pacifist and indefatigable worker in the hip community. He has come to prepare a delicious macrobiotic meal for whoever is hungry. He arrives every day in the late afternoon. He is part of the phenomenon that is San Francisco.

The Straight Theatre is offered for free performances, its two young spokesmen assuring us that if contributions from the performances can't support the company, free food can probably be arranged with Bay Area communes. "This theatre is liberated territory," they assert with enviable pride. They want *Frankenstein* and *Antigone, no Paradise.* They were miles ahead already.

The first day in San Francisco, the beginning of a love affair with the most beautiful city in America.

On the second day it is learned that, bowing to pressure applied on behalf of the Living Theatre (the most influential faction said to be educational channel KQED which has arranged for a videotaping of parts of *Mysteries*), the management of the Nourse Auditorium has agreed to open its doors for the scheduled performances. In order to fulfill this commitment, the company must bow out of its agreement with the representatives of the hip community at the Straight Theatre, and in so doing, a certain amount of resentment arises from that quarter, despite Julian's having explained from the start that such was possible and why it would be necessary that the company accept it. Nevertheless, the Living are put down for not rejecting the commercial theatre that had initially rejected them because they want money. Hoping to restore compatible relations with the Hashbury, the Living promises a free performance of *Mysteries* for Sunday afternoon in Golden Gate Park and another one of *Paradise* Monday night at the Straight. Nonetheless, the move to the Nourse tends to alienate the sympathies of the hip community, although some of its leaders do come out to see *Frankenstein* and *Antigone.* It should be noted

185

here that on the first night in San Francisco the Living had appeared at the Straight for what was originally to be a free performance of *Paradise,* but what on second thought, after a quick reading of the prevailing condition by those who had arranged the event, was reconsidered as an "opening party" for the Living. But more on that later. Back to the Nourse. . . .

Where shows go on without government intervention, an accord having been reached between it and the company's legal and accounting representatives in New York whereby the balance of the tax bill will be paid out of proceeds from the final engagement at the Brooklyn Academy of Music before the European departure. However, every night the box office receipts are seized by Carl Einhorn and held by Julian to ensure that the Living will be paid the salaries in arrears, minus the $5 daily allotment which remains in effect until they leave California, and to make sure there is money for the return fares to Europe. *Paradise* attracts its most serious attention from a fire marshal. The Nourse engagement is otherwise uneventful; this most European of American cities is willingly given the upper hand for this visitor's attention.

The afternoon sun slanting over Golden Gate Park, washing its westward face of Stanyon Street and casting long shadows down Haight. Haight-Asbury, the crossroad in the Golden Age of the flower scene, now a littered trail staked out by "speed" merchants and the "hard" dealers of the death trip. The Golden Age is over . . . its demise duly reported by the

186

mass press, which had prematurely induced its birth to begin with; functioning as it does three months ahead of the world, invention was the mother. Of necessity. And little wonder it had died. And in its grim aftermath, a proliferation of "head" shops stands in resolute tackiness among iron-gated cross-hatched out-of-businesses whose merchandise hangs in faded testimony to the principle that economics, as always, is a matter of supply and demand.

LSD, THC, STP, DMT . . . : the alphabetized chemistry of space travel.

Horse, meth, cocaine . . . : the hard sell.

Acid, mescaline, peyote . . . : the visionary profiteers.

Voices murmuring through lips that do not move; the sunken socketed eyes of Haight . . . the pavement symphony counterpointed by the gotta-penny panhandlers slouching on the down side of the trip; shadowy figures huddled in doorways, seeking shelter from the cold night air; zomboid bodies, faces haunted by the fury of two many psychic demons unleashed too many times, too many combinations of too many Miracle Drugs. The climate of Haight: discomforting, violent, heavy with a corrosive sense of paranoia. PORTLAND, ST. LOUIS, PALM SPRINGS, NEW YORK, to Anywhere from Nowhere, the crayonned signs at freeway entrances and the joyless gaze at cars that do not stop. Getting there was all the fun.

"Flower children," "hippies," "psychedelic" . . . in 1967 the mass press had zenned in on the Hashbury tableau, explaining that these colorful young people were actually involved, in reality, that is, in the doing of their thing . . .

whatever that meant. Mass press always covered its tracks with occasional innuendoes and frequent riffs concerning The Use of Drugs. In case its readers mistook the conception to be immaculate.

Brief and possibly irrelevant flashback to the spring of 1968: Having peaked on the West Coast, the Golden Age has radiated one of its most powerful and durable beams, the Jefferson Airplane, into a press conference at Hunter College, New York City, where the following terse exchange takes place amidst a clamor of high school newspaper reporters, a caution of TV, radio, and press representatives, and a full-gaggle of hard-pressed agents, managers, and so forth for the Airplane:

Eager High-School Reporter: Is it true that you take drugs?

There is a brief pause as Airplane attendant Bill Graham fidgets with the tilt of his microphone, a press agent from RCA-Victor tries to pretend he's not there, and the Airplane look as if they've been there and left already. Then:

Member of the Airplane: You don't take drugs; they take you.

A smattering of laughter from the press section. Not because the question has been fielded with any particular cleverness, but because it had been posed in the first place. The interview was soon restored to its do-you-sleep-in-the-nude level of erudition, and no one gave second thought to the crass interruption of the pimply faced news-climber.

No one involved in it had ever denied that the San Francisco scene was a drug-oriented culture, and only those con-

188

cerned with marketing it to the masses were about to. If music was its most marketable commodity, it was also its most vital, but it was also something more than that. In a sense the San Francisco rock groups were a tactical reconnaissance troupe that infiltrated the American mass pop enclave, electrifying it . . . turning it on, as it were . . . with a coded message more profound than anything else that emerged from the flower scene . . . for when the code was broken, a revolution had taken place.

A revolution which, due to unexpected but perhaps inevitable setbacks and interference from elements new to its milieu, would be slowed down before the next step could be taken. For in the spring of 1969 Michael Itkin speaks of violence and crime in the Hashbury and others echo his concern: the "speed" merchants have moved in, the "hard" drug pushers have arrived; addiction has become a problem among the young people in the community. The psychedelic, consciousness-expanding, non-addictive drugs had always been the avowed orientation. Even its most zealous public opposition to the increasing use of such substances had been careful to stress the physiological differences, but ultimately the publicity engulfing the Hashbury served only to work against it. The curious young people continued to pour in, late-comers with nothing to do, no place to go, the ready marks for the newly entrenched "hard" drug pushers. When the money ran out, they became the murmuring sidewalk shills and panhandlers. The cycle of crime began again, addiction, theft, violence. . . .

And yet for all the ugliness and debris in the aftermath of the flower-love experience, the Hashbury today is somewhere else, moving in a positive direction toward the next stage of the revolution. There exists a stronger, deeper-rooted sense of community than before, a determined effort to pick up the pieces and continue. The street reality, unavoidable, depressing, debilitating in its tension, is in a perverse sense a *superficial reality,* a surface wound in a slow and uncertain process of healing, for beneath its blight the community is reassembling and moving together with energy and vitality, with a beautiful force that is not generated by tension.

Unique, since it remains quite openly a drug-oriented culture; it has advanced so far ahead in other areas that drugs are no longer an important issue. No longer "hippie" but a hip community, the Hashbury has assumed a more responsible social and creative commitment. More politically alert and involved now, its alignment holds a greater viability in terms of the liberated life style it is dedicated to bringing about. Despite the visible squalor of its street life, contrary to all negative observations, mine and others', on Haight Street Revisited, the Hashbury is not a ghetto . . . it is a more urbanized, and therefore more constricted, reflection of the affirmative collective movement within the radicalized Bay Area. The ultimate objective is a permanent Golden Age. And the destination is clear.

A Word or Two About Chromosomal Damage

The free performances at the Straight Theatre are best summed up in Space To The Spaced, the manifesto of what in the very loosest of terms could be designated as The Audience. Apparently drawing the hospitality line at the basic essentials of food, shelter, and a copious cornucopia of drugs, the Hashbury residents made it quite clear that they could not be imposed upon to put their skin on and watch their guests perform. Just as well, because The Audience was definitely the show. The Straight atmosphere is difficult to describe beyond the speculation that it would probably be the end result if Burroughs and R. Crumb collaborated on the Apocalypse. It is a roiling pit of unbridled dementia, and yet there is something oddly *convivial* about it, a sort of flashed-out affability that exudes a comforting sensation that brain damage can be fun.

On their first visit, sensing something to that effect, the Living had finally opted for getting down with the action and not disturbing the pandemonium, a shrewd gesture prompted to a great extent by a missing alternative. The option was prefaced by some discussion as to what part or how much of *Paradise* could be done—the Living do not give up so easily; however, it was a foregone conclusion that the whole thing would not be tolerated—and it was eventually decided to do only the Mat Piece, a brilliant example of editing-under-fire, since the mat piece is part of the Rite of Opposite Forces on the Sixth Rung. Having settled that, the next problem was where to find space among the few hundred spaced to do it. The solution for this was a technique called the *metaphysical jungle:* starting from scattered points around the theatre, the actors move through the crowd toward a preappointed rendezvous location, in this case near the center of the room; moving slowly but purposely, eyes focused straight ahead, a resonant hum, a "Chord," rises from their collective bodies as they converge at the point of action;

there they wait as "The Chord" subsides, pause, and then the action begins. It was a technique used in situations similar to the present one, not only to clear a space in which to perform but also to quiet the audience and prepare it for what was to follow. It worked with varying degrees of success, depending upon the disorderliness of the given crowd, and this time it worked only insofar as it did manage to clear a small area in which the brief performance could take place. The performance itself, the mat piece, did not drastically alter the general Straight atmosphere; however, it did affect those in the immediate vicinity and created a small but crowded pocket of attention, a gentling vibration that spread slowly into the peripheral regions, soothing if not silencing them. As the tone gradually changed, it was soon evident that it would not be strong enough to affect the farther reaches of the theatre, and before the piece was finished they had rushed in again as if to fill a vacuum. The Living had made a worthwhile effort and had succeeded, if only temporarily, and they left as the maelstrom was being restored to its fullest intensity.

That first night would be the "best" of the three Hashbury performances. Golden Gate Park, specifically a location dubbed "Hippie Hill," was to be the setting for *Mysteries* on a Sunday afternoon. Set to begin at one o'clock, it never happened because (1) the Living arrived at three, and (2) eight rock groups were playing in concert just over the Hill. But Hippie Hill was by no means vacant. Hippie Hill would be the end result of a Burroughs-Crumb collaboration with the Fresh Air Fund. The last of the Hashbury no-show shows, the Straight again on the last night in San Francisco.

192

Mysteries, once again for the first time; this time the company got as far as the Brig Dollar, the opening piece. When the Hashbury goes to the theatre it's a tough act to follow.

If company morale had been low at other times, it became virtually nonexistent now with the worsening money problem and the uncertainty of the tour. Somewhere between Berkeley and Los Angeles something had snapped from the pressure. No longer a closely knit community, they seemed to be drifting helplessly away from each other, yet clutching at one another with a quiet desperation because there was nowhere else to go. The Presence, that feeling of oneness so impressive in the beginning, dissolved into the one common interest that could still be shared and communicated: drugs. This was hardly a new interest, nor a particularly unique one these days, as there was little question of drugs having helped in illuminating many facets of their collective creativity. These were consciousness-expanding drugs, the nonaddictive psychedelics, and they were taken casually, literally and figuratively speaking, and the company had learned to work behind these substances in an admirable way that contributed much to the magical effect of their work.

But after Berkeley, as circumstances grew increasingly worse, the farther was the retreat from an abundant supply of—it must be said as one compliments a chef—truly excellent "head" drugs to local specialties strongly laced with "hard" drugs. It was unusual to see the escapist alcoholic-junky syndrome applied to "head" drugs, but such were either very cheap (compared to elsewhere) or given free, and it's difficult to support a "hard" addiction on five dollars a day. Five-a-day keeps the monkey away. But as escapism took hold, experimentation began with weird combinations of "head" and "hard," the ultimate achievement being removal rather than reasonable distance from reality. As the relentless investigation took its toll in sickness and fucked-up heads, the performances became miraculous rather than magical. On the last night in San Francisco the back salaries for the past couple of weeks, minus the five-dollar daily allotments, would be paid, and in most cases it would go immediately into inexpensive though sizable nest-eggs that would hold the company through the horrors of the bus ride back east.

Julian would take care of the reality bag; he would take care of everything and make it nice. Kiss it and make it well. Julian would see that they were fed and housed and got to ride on the big bus with Tony . . . a cage that held them together while driving them apart through confinement that made them rage at each other, that through its insularity made them totally dependent upon each other. It was a bestiary of exotic creatures, an impressive array of mindlessly obedient encumbrances. It was safer . . . no, easier . . . to follow Papa Julian than to jeopardize things with a responsible attitude, even toward oneself. Julian was Hannibal leading his elephants over the Alps.

There were exceptions, of course, those who out of disillusionment and a sense of frustration chose to go their own way as best they could, and some were beautiful creatures, each in his own distinct style . . . for the beautiful ones had style, a reflection of certain shared characteristics: intelligence and sensitivity and a strong sense of identity.

They stood for what the entire Living Theatre should have
been, or would be if it only had the guts to jettison the dead
weight that counterfeited its value with ignorance and irresponsibility. For the beautiful ones the laborious journey
was a rite of passage, the aftermath of which would leave
them stronger than before. Perhaps they understood that
this monstrous thing that was America, for all its glaring
and unforgivable deformities, for all that it may destroy
in them, was an experience that had to be undergone with
resilience, because it had to be taken on its own precarious
terms. For with all its ugliness and waste, it contained within
it a melange of energies that were at once its saving grace
(its very nature was movement) and the cause of its terrible
conflicts (every movement brought a countermovement).
This monstrous America had never come to terms with
itself and probably never would. For the life of it.

Even if the Living Theatre had been at its best, it still would
have run into trouble in Berkeley and San Francisco because
of conflicting political stances between it and those communities. The Living Theatre was placed in a defensive
position which its low morale coupled with the fact that it
was no longer functioning as a unit made it incapable of sur-
mounting. As far as the public was concerned, the Becks,
namely Julian here, were the official spokesmen for the
company, and despite Julian's noble convictions and the
lucidity accompanying their articulation, there had always
been an element of improbability in his methods for achieving the ultimate goals of a cultural revolution. Repetition
made his words seem platitudinous, particularly now when

195

it was obvious that the Bay Area form of radicalism was decidedly more relevant and perfectly attuned to the immediacy evolving from its commitment.

Intelligent, aware, and impatient with the political pieties of the Becks, Rufus Collins spoke out in support of the community's position and called for a more realistic approach on the part of the company. With little support from the rest of the company, he persisted in an attempt to move them to a position from which they could be taken seriously and to change *Paradise* in ways that would give it the pertinence it needed now more than ever before. It was a futile effort to make Julian see that these changes were vital.

In continuing to speak for the Living Theatre, Julian became increasingly stubborn, adamant in his refusal to make changes either in *Paradise* or in what was presumed to be the collective ideology of the group, and he clung protectively to a position that showed itself to be somewhat old-fashioned, indeed romantic. It was challenged not only by Rufus but by the young and not-so-young who had respected the art of the company, but having argued patiently with its political point of view, they left with an attitude of I-Love-you-Baby but shut-up. The spectre of Ronnie Johnson was always close, a somewhat less formidable but equally clear reverberation of that September afternoon back in New Haven, and through it all, one could imagine him saying: See, I told you so. Except that you knew that the Ronnie Johnsons had more important scores to check out.

As demonstrations on campuses across the country continued well into the spring, an occasional dean would utter words to the effect that such were due to the influence of the

196

Living Theatre, and to them it may have appeared a plausible explanation for the outbreaks that did seem to follow the itinerary from Madison to Reed. It was purely coincidence: the Living Theatre simply had not been taken seriously by radical elements in America, collegiate or otherwise. Its naïveté on the crucial point of nonviolence, particularly in the repetition of its phrasing, had been regarded as a theatrical device by those who were earnestly into the revolution.

It would be misleading to assume that the real issue was whether or not to change the script of *Paradise,* for *Paradise* was merely the instrument for getting at something more essential and far more important in terms of the struggle in which both sides were committed to the same objective: to the creation of what Julian called the "bearable world." The issue was violence, though both sides fundamentally agreed that it wasn't a beneficial means toward the mutual goal. The divisive difference was that Julian . . . and by extension the Living Theatre and all pacifists . . . rejected outright the resort to violence for any reason or under any provocation, while his challengers accepted it as a necessary measure under certain sets of circumstances in which retaliation was the only answer to dangerous provocation. Those who questioned the tenets of passive resistance recognized a need to prepare *against* violence, a less abstract code that tended to existentialize martyrdom. As a dialectic both positions are ultimately meaningless because they are premature, and practical application of either point of view is totally dependent upon The Emergency, whatever form it takes. When the aim is the same the vital thing is alignment, rather than further alienation among those who are tired of alienation and seeking to resolve it.

The Becks' point of view and blind faith in the Love Zap are not without their ironies and contradictions. Though they preferred to ignore it, many of the Living had taken an active part in the Avignon riots at the time of the Theatre Festival in July of 1968. A retaliatory participation, it had been necessitated when the lives of the women and children were endangered by a mob that invaded the ancient building that housed the company. The actors fought through the night and succeeded in forcing the assailants from the besieged structure. It was not a matter of heroics, but an action required for the safety of those trapped inside the building. But their action was violent, and therefore shameful. A similar attitude exists in relation to those few of the company who took an active part in the May riots in Paris.

Yet there is pride in the Living Theatre's involvement in both events, the implication being that the entire company should be given full credit, particularly for the less violent occupation of the Odeon Theatre. In the course of lectures and interviews along the American tour, the Becks frequently prefaced remarks concerning the events of Paris and Avignon with: "Of course, it would be presumptuous of us to say that the Living Theatre was responsible for the French revolution. . . ." Perhaps it would.

Beneath the company's vociferous proclamations of nonviolence ran an undercurrent of hostility, a psychological violence in the way they dealt with each other and in the various methods of individual catharsis, both onstage and off, that were generally held to be virtues, but which too often

revealed themselves to be head-twisting games and verbal
flagellation, confrontation tactics used to cop-out for not
having an honest response. Depending on the mentality
involved, these defenses ran the gamut from run-of-the-mill
wise-ass remarks to cleverly disguised psychological warfare,
the Becks being past masters of the latter form. I recall two
private conversations with Judith in which I was the subject,
or object, and on both occasions . . . one in Philadelphia,
the other in Appleton, Wisconsin . . . I had gotten the impression that her outburst was something she was putting
herself through in order to feel better afterward. I had
weathered the storms in the hope of finding something useful in the debris, but the pickings were sparse, nothing that
could readily be converted into anything particularly worthwhile. I remember that after both meetings I had returned
to my room and fallen asleep from the fatigue of the quest—
which may have been the objective, in which case the tactics
are beneficial.

On the other hand, Judith could be totally candid in regard to herself and direct in a way that most women aren't,
because most women are embarrassed by honesty, and there
was an unexpected vulnerability beneath the toughness, and
I liked her when those qualities were leveled through the
games. More important though, *Antigone* had instilled an
unwavering respect and admiration and the rest was in-
consequential. This too is not without its irony, for in another
part of her complex character was the romantic desire to be
seriously regarded as an actress in the classical tradition of
Duse. As an actress, Judith is a brilliant director.

Not even the Becks' overworked sense of destiny could

pull the company together in the acid test of San Francisco. The tour had succeeded through the Living Theatre's considerable theatrical merits, but it had failed profoundly by insisting that its ideology receive equal, preferably more, time. When stripped of its powerful artistic facade, the bare ideology was a dubious structure that appeared to be fixed in place by sheer tenacity and by the tension of supporting the two elements. In defending the Living's political precepts, there was often a tendency to rationalize, to edit the immediate situation, keeping that which served the collective image, or what could be reinterpreted to serve it, while turning away from that which remained relentlessly opposed to it. Often, not always. Julian in a lecture in Ann Arbor:

"We are forty people, dependent for our livelihood on a certain situation. In the highest revolutionary sense, this is obsolete."

Through this comes a clearer perspective on the nature of the Living Theatre as a communal entity. Through its peripatetic existence, moving from place to place, country to country, nomadic, unrooted . . . and thereby exotic . . . a distance was imposed that isolated it from all environments, from all other communal entities, and prevented it from relating directly to or involving itself completely in the prevailing conditions and struggles of any given community. Despite its revolutionary nature, the parallel culture held a deep sense of environmental permanence and had to confront the immediate, the real necessities and dangers as it struggled toward the ultimate objectives. The Living Theatre was always a community in transit and could therefore

200

hold to an ideological commitment that refused to be particularized in terms of the immediate situation; its commitment could be interpreted as superficial, as escape rather than liberation.

The immediate situation: the revolution.

"By any means necessary": Bobby Seale.

Paradise Now

Between January 31 and February 9 of 1968 four rehearsal sessions took place in Rome to begin working toward the realization of an idea that had been with the company for over a year. Until Rome nothing had been determined except that a completely new step would be taken and that it would be called *Paradise Now*. On February 19 of that year the Living Theatre arrived in Cefalù, Sicily, where it would stay until the end of April; what developed within this period was the Mat Piece and the Totem Poles, components of the original version which at that time was based on a ten-rung map. The real work began in Avignon, France, from May 21 to July 24, and there *Paradise Now* was pulled together into the eight-rung final version.

Hours, days, weeks of talking, theorizing, note-taking and long rehearsals that had to be fitted into what time remained after rehearsals and performances of *Antigone* at the 1968 Theatre Festival of Avignon: *Paradise* premiered at that festival on July 24 and what emerged was a revolutionary piece that liberated itself from all theatrical "methods" and ideas that had gone before, while proclaiming irreverently that "theatre" was, yes . . . *in the street,* and thereby implying a need to destroy its own reason for being.

Paradise had sprung from three basic concepts:

1. The need to destroy the theatrical form forever; *Mysteries, Frankenstein,* and *Antigone* had not been enough, for the total alienation of the bourgeoisie contained the real art vs. life experience.

2. The need to show the *alternative; The Brig, The Maids, Mysteries, Frankenstein,* and *Antigone* presented only the horrors, denunciations (or refusals) without resolution. Work must begin to find the alternative.

3. The mystical and political aspirations of the company.

Prior to the American tour, between the July premiere and the end of August, *Paradise* had played a total of eight performances in Avignon and Geneva. These performances were characterized by the presence of audiences with a highly revolutionary collective consciousness. The language barrier, only partially overcome by the actors, worked *from* the spectators, creating a distance from which would evolve a more restrained but extremely aware participation, a reaction that was less random and neither as superficial nor as irrational as that which was to characterize American audiences. In Europe it had been necessary and possible for the actors to express themselves in a magic-Artaudian, nonverbal idiom; in America, language games and intellectual competition were able to develop so that the spectator became an adversary who had to be overcome, beaten down and shaken up in order to convey a message of truth and honesty. Consequently, the spectator continued to arm himself against the message, and *Paradise* became a confrontation of assault and counterassault in which the actors had to try to affect the audience on a subconscious level where

204

a reaction would not be immediate but would work, hope-fully, by a delayed feedback.

In America, *Paradise* had the aura of involuntary suicide, like aiming a pistol at someone and having it explode in your hand, and its best performances were usually in places where the Becks or others in the company had lectured before-hand, creating more respect and serious attention by ex-plaining its intent. But most often such gatherings could not be arranged, and the audience's only "preparation" was the tremendous publicity and controversy surrounding it, a fore-cast that told them it was a freak show in which they could take over and do what they wanted to do. Mistakenly con-vinced that audience participation was permitted in all the Living Theatre's work, the other plays were sometimes dis-rupted if *Paradise* played earlier in a run. A "controlled happening," the Actions had been designed expressly for the spectator-participants and it encouraged their complete freedom to act and do whatever they wished. However, neither the actors nor the structure of the piece had been prepared for the aggressive young audiences it would find in America and for those who believed that confrontation was the only real method of communication. It became a dangerous game that allowed those with a stronger ego to take control and determine the pattern of the entire show.

If its bold form and sublime aspirations over-reached its intellectual capacity, *Paradise* was nevertheless an effort that had never been attempted before. Intellectually pretentious and self-indulgent as it all too often was . . . and tedious as it always was . . . its conceptualized function and the structure in which it had been conceived made it unique. It was a magnificent failure that could only be compared to itself, whose quality was relative only in terms of one *Paradise Now* being better or worse than another experience that had also been called *Paradise Now*.

The following is the unrevised version of the text for the preparation of *Paradise Now,* a collective creation of the Living Theatre, transcribed from a tape made by the Becks:

This play is a voyage from the Many to the One and from the One to the Many. It is a spiritual voyage and a political voyage; it is an interior voyage and an exterior voyage. It is a voyage for the actors and for the spectator. It begins in the present and moves into the future and returns to the present. The chart is the map. To prepare for the voyage, the performance, the actors should make a study of anarchist philosophy and of the various spiritual and metaphysical teachings.

The chart depicts a ladder of eight rungs, a vertical ascent toward permanent revolution. Each rung consists of a Rite, a Vision, and an Action, which lead to the fulfillment of an aspect of the revolution. The Rites and Visions are performed primarily by the actors, but the Actions are introduced by the actors and performed by the spectators with the help of the actors. The Actions are introduced by a text spoken by the actors; the Rites are fundamentally physical, spiritual, ritual ceremonies which culminate in a flash-out; the Visions are essentially intellectual images, symbols, dreams enacted by the actors. The Actions are an enactment by the spectators of political conditions. These conditions are specified as taking place in a particular city, but they lead to revolutionary action for the here and now.

The revolution of which the play speaks is the beautiful nonviolent anarchist revolution.

The chart contains information drawn from the Kabala, from Tantric literature, the *I Ching* and various other doctrines. All of the information on the chart is arranged as a vertical ascent. The purpose of the play is to lead to a state of being in which nonviolent revolutionary action is possible.

206

RUNG ONE

The Rite of Guerilla Theatre

The audience is almost completely assembled when the actors enter the theatre and mingle with the spectators, in the aisles, on stage, in the lobby. Each actor approaches a spectator and addresses him individually in a voice that is very quiet, urgent, but personal in feeling. The actor speaks the first of five phrases: *"I'm not allowed to travel without a passport."* Going from spectator to spectator, he repeats this phrase and *only* this phrase, each repetition expressing greater urgency and frustration, for he is obsessed with its meaning and ramifications; he cannot travel freely, cannot move at will, we are separated by artificial boundaries. Shouting the words with anguish and frustration, the energies surge to a point of near-hysteria as the actors go beyond words and into a collective scream. It is the revolutionary outcry. Flash-out.

The return to the artist's quiet center, they stand motionless, breathing. Pause. The second phrase begins: *"I don't know how to stop the wars."* Again directed to the individual spectator, the passion mounts; the violence and killing continue because no one knows how to stop it. The crescendo of the collective scream, the flash-out. Pause. Phrase three: *"You can't live if you don't have money";* creative energy must be wasted in competition for material gain. Crescendo. Scream. Flash-out. Phrase four: *"I'm not allowed to smoke marijuana";* repressive laws control our minds and prohibit the exploration of deeper consciousness. Crescendo. Scream. Flash-out. Phrase five: *"I'm not allowed to take my clothes off";* sexual

207

repression has twisted our minds, our bodies are ugly, sex is over-shadowed by guilt. Anguish, frustration crescendoes . . . but the actors *do not* scream. Instead they remove all of their clothing down to costumes that expose only as much of their bodies as is *legally permissible;* they are *not* allowed to take their clothes off. Flash-out.

The Vision of the Death and Resurrection of the American Indian

The actors gather on stage in a ceremonial circle, and sitting cross-legged, they smoke the pipe of peace and pass it among themselves. Flash-out. Then, one by one, they rise and take positions for five Totem Poles, each consisting of four actors . . . the bottom man crouching low, the second standing behind him with his legs spread wide, and behind him, the third man carrying the fourth on his shoulders . . . in various totemistic, animistic positions and facial expressions. They stand motionless and then begin to advance slowly, beating a rhythm with their feet; the emergence of the natural man. As they advance, they are shot down one by one, making the sound of the bullet and screaming as they fall forward, face-down on the stage: the image of the slain red man.

Action: The lines are distributed among the actors and delivered from their prone position on the stage. The text calls for the spectator to act, feel free, and express various political points of view that would enact the culture, undo it, and change it. They pause at the end of the text and wait for the audience to react. After one minute the actors, still lying face-down, begin to beat the rhythm of an Indian dance on the floor with their knees, and at the appropriate time a chant begins: *If I could turn you on, if I could drive you out of your wretched mind, if I could tell you, I would let you know.*[1]

It is taken up by all of the actors, who then begin to rise and dance exultantly, out into the audience, up the aisles, as the chant continues. Flash-out. It is supposed to represent the hippie culture rising in reincarnation of the American Indian, aspiring to be the natural man, the great suppressed culture. The assault from below is the first revolutionary action to change the culture; the natural man knows he can travel without a passport, that he can live without money, take his clothes off and so forth. He confronts the spectator with the challenge to join him.

[1]Ronald Laing, *The Politics of Experience.*

RUNG TWO

The Rite of Prayer

The Holies; the actor moves slowly, quietly from person to person whispering two words of praise either about his person ("holy hand"), an article of his clothing ("holy shirt"), or an object in the room ("holy chair"). He speaks softly and touches the spectator gently. It is a prayer in praise of the sacredness and universal identification of all things.

The Vision of the Discovery of the North Pole

The text begins: "This polar expedition took four years to prepare and will take sixteen months to complete. It is one of the most difficult and challenging journeys left to be made by man on this planet." With shivering sound and gestures of struggling against arctic winds and snow, the actors have taken positions to begin the journey to the North Pole, which is formed by five actors in the center of the stage and revolves slowly while emitting an electromagnetic sound. From two lines that have formed in the side-aisles, the other actors are cartwheeled on stage where they form three spokes radiating from the Pole. The central figure of the pole holds his arms outstretched and begins the text which is continued until all the actors have spun into the revolving configuration. When they have reached the Pole, its central figure asks: "Where are you?" The first actor spins off answering: "Here I am." The Pole asks: "How long will you live?" Another actor spins off and replies: "It is time to revolt." The Pole asks: "What do you want?" As the actors spin off one by one from the revolving spokes they answer, stating the goals of the revolution: "To feed all the people," "To work for the love of it and not for the money," "To stop wasting the planet," and so on.

Finally the Pole asks: "What is this called?" With their bodies, the actors spell out the word ANARCHISM.

The Pole asks: "What is anarchism?" The bodies spell out the word PARADISE and chant "Now!"

This is a vision of finding the center, of crystallization and clarification, of spelling it out. It is the vision of making the difficult journey in order to find the answer; by being asked the right ques-

209

tion, we find the right answer. The discovery of the axis of the world. The scene is physically difficult to perform.

Action: Bolivia . . . Free theatre. What is to be done? . . . How the Rite of Prayer and the vision of the Discovery of the Discovery of the North Pole can lead to the revolution of revelation . . .

The text is delivered as the actors break from the formation of PARADISE and move into the audience and wait for it to take up the revolutionary theme of this Rung. The purpose of Rung Two is to plan the nonviolent revolution, and the actors play out the action initiated by the audience. As with all of the Actions, there is no time and it goes on until the actors feel that its content has been exhausted.

RUNG THREE

The Rite of Study

Seated cross-legged in a circle in the center of the stage, the actors face each other and perform a series of improvised gestures (*mudras*) and phrases (*mantras*). The *mudras* are executed with the arms and hands only, and the energy generated by this action produces the *mantras*, the invented phrases that begin with "To be free"; examples: to be free is to be free to eat; to be free is to be free of money; to be free is to be free of violence,—of the system, —of prejudice,—of hatred, et cetera. When a certain intensity is reached, the actors stop and hold the position of the last *mudra,* at which point the audience may join in and invent *mantras.* The performers hold their positions until the audience finishes. Flash-out.

The Vision of the Creation of Life

The performers rise from their *mudra* positions and, with eyes closed, start to move slowly, lifelessly, each individual having no connection with any other. As they move, one will touch another by chance, and these two will begin to move together more cohesively, but they will not become lifelike until five bodies, five elements, have come together by accident. At this point a change occurs, and they begin to move and function as one organic entity, reaching, touching,

210

relating to each other's bodies and to the space between them: they have opened their eyes now and are making a sound of the sea, of life, a sound that becomes more resonant as the movements continue. Taking each other's hands, in circles of five, they raise their arms and make an exultant sound. It is the vision of unification and life-giving force; the elemental structure of the cell, a pattern for social structure.

Action: Initiated by the audience, the theme of this rung is to instigate the gathering of revolutionary forces. The action is supposed to refer to the city in which the performance is taking place, to the here and now. Based upon information gathered beforehand (hopefully), the text is altered in accordance with the actual social and political situation existing in the given community.

RUNG FOUR

The Rite of Universal Intercourse

The actors lie down together in the center of the playing area, their bodies forming a pile, caressing, undulating, each performer reaching out toward any or all bodies that touch him: breaking the touch barrier. As the bodies move together, a low hum is emitted. If two performers are closely drawn to each other, they may separate themselves from the body-pile and sit close by it in the *maithuna* position . . . one sits cross-legged while the other sits facing him (or her; either position can be assumed by a member of either sex) with legs encircling his waist. There is very little movement; it is a form of deep physical absorption and communication. They may return to the group and return later to the *maithuna* position if they wish, together or with someone else if they wish.

The Vision of Apokatastasis

The actors rise from the Rite of Universal Intercourse and pair off in positions of Victim and Executioner: the Executioner stands with his back to the audience, his right hand extended toward the head of the Victim with a finger pointing in children's representation of a

211

gun. The Victim stands with his hands behind his back facing the audience.[2] In unison, the Executioners make the sound of the firing of a gun; the Victims fall simultaneously. The Victims rise again and resume their original position; the Executioners fire. Victims rise, Executioners fire: it is repeated twenty times. At the end of these enactments the Victims begin to address the Executioners with the words of the Rite of Prayer ("holy face," "holy eye") and the Executioners respond with the words of the Rite of Guerilla Theatre ("I'm not allowed to travel without a passport," etc.). The Executioners continue to fire, the Victims to fall; the respective words are repeated until the Executioner responds with love and the two embrace. Flash-out. Image: the reversal, the transformation of the demonic forces into the celestial; Apokatastasis.

Action: The text here develops the idea that sexual taboos and the touch barrier divide men and are the source of violence. The destruction of these taboos and barriers will transform the demonic forces into the celestial; the sexual revolution furthers the nonviolent revolution, because before the sexual revolution the energy is violent. This Action ends with a second Rite of Universal Intercourse (body pile) and this time members of the audience are encouraged to take part.

RUNG FIVE

The Rite of the Mysterious Voyage (The Flip-Out)

As the actors rise from the Rite of Universal Intercourse and begin to move away, one actor remains in the center and begins to make a sound, a sound of possession by dark forces. The actors form a circle around him, watching him and assisting him in his voyage, which consists of a self-induced trancelike state. It is painful, and he moves around making sounds and gestures that rise from his internal experience. The others respond, breathing, moving, and

[2]The position approximates a photograph in the *New York Times,* January 1968 showing the execution of a Viet Cong by a South Vietnamese officer.

212

making sounds with him, sometimes they come close and touch him, sometimes they just circle him; they are taking the energy from his voyage, from his private experience, and making it a communal energy and experience. As his trance reaches an explosive intensity the others follow in sound-and-movement and gradually begin to transform his action into a positive action that becomes less painful and difficult. His movements gradually become fluid and beautiful, the sound joyous.

The principle of the self-induced trance is to allow pain and tantrum and madness to possess one, to push into dangerous psychic areas and flow with these demonic forces without holding back. One must confront the unknown, for only then will the dark forces be obviated; one returns from the voyage in a highly charged state. It is an act of purification. Flash-out.

The actor who has taken the voyage gives a signal to the others, to the community, indicating his Here and Now.

The Vision of the Integration of the Races

The actors gather in the performing area and move about exchanging hostile looks; everyone stops. One turns to another and says "Jew"; the Jew replies, "Christian." They look at each other with deep hostility, then turn and move quickly to opposite sides of the area. This is repeated using the same appellations until all of the actors stand facing each other in two camps, which then move toward each other slowly with hostile looks and a manner of suppressed violence. In the center they mingle again and then stop. The same process is repeated using black-white, young-old, and short-tall. The performers then turn outward from the playing area and begin to address individuals in the audience with these appellations, eventually extending the name-calling from the more or less appropriate to the absurd (surrealist, monkey, Martian, etc.). As the words change into absurd epithets, the tone becomes less hostile, the approach becomes friendly, joking and foolish, and the relationship becomes affectionate and tender. The performer then begins to address the spectator as Thou, indicating himself as I. I-Thou; he continues, mixing them sometimes, indicating himself as Thou, the other as I. Flash-out.

213

Action: The theme of this rung is the enactment of the revolution of action, the change from the preparatory stage to the revolutionary stage. From this point on, the play's action takes place in time-future. It is the work of the actors to guide the public into a projection of the revolutionary situation.

RUNG SIX

The Rite of Opposite Forces (The Mat Piece)

When the preceding Action has culminated, an actor lies down in the center of the area. He relaxes his mind and his body; his body is limp, his mind in free space. Breathing deeply and fully, he makes a loud steady sound as the other actors encircle him. Singly or in groups of two or more the others approach and perform certain ritual actions on him . . . they touch, caress, lift, shake, strike, and stroke him; they move his hair and his limbs; they kiss him, they make sounds in his ears, on his face and on various parts of his body; they turn his body in various positions, using it in different ways. They approach him and perform all of their actions with tremendous energy, bringing both positive and negative forces which they try to pass into the body of the central subject. They try to rouse him from his passivity and divert him from his quiet center. By accepting these forces and remaining in a fully receptive state, the subject holds his center and maintains his passive state, and all energy released toward him charges him and takes him on a trip which at its conclusion has transformed him and released him in a state of transcendent energy. Flash-out. The subject rises and signals of his Here and Now.

The Vision of the Magic Love Zap

The actors form a configuration which is supposed to represent a pentagon within which a large statue of Mammon is made by five actors. In front of the statue a Victim lies spread-eagled on the floor in a sacrificial position; four priests stand behind the statue. The actors forming the walls of the pentagon assume the fierce poses of the guardian statues of Eastern temples or the gargoyles of Western

214

churches. At a signal the temple doors open, and the actors stamp outward to reveal the inside of the pentagon. When the gates are opened the priests move from behind the statue, slashing the air with knives as they approach the Victim. They raise their knives and plunge toward the Victim, but they are magically deflected in mid-air by the Victim, who then rises toward them offering his throat. The actors' hands change from the gestures indicating a knife to gestures of blessing. The priests bless the Victim. It is a vision of the nonviolent conquest of the Pentagon. Black-out.

Action: The reference here is to the period of revolutionary struggle that follows the revolution of action. It raises the problem which the revolutionaries must face when the reactionary forces try to destroy their accomplishments with force and violence. The question is, How does the nonviolent revolutionary overcome? The Action continues as long as the energy sustains it.

RUNG SEVEN

The Rite of New Possibilities

In the darkness that follows the above Action, the performers experiment with their voice boxes and vocal chords, reaching as far as they can toward the creation of new sounds and sound relationships that are not within their usual conscious range of sound. They listen to each other and play on each other's energy patterns.

The Vision of the Landing on Mars

The theatre is still dark as five actors move slowly from the rear in a formation arranged to represent a spaceship. They carry small lights or lanterns. Actors representing the moon, Mars, Saturn, Pluto, and a galaxy rotate slowly through the theatre. They too are carrying small lights and lanterns, and the body of the actor playing the galaxy is strung with small lights so that when he moves he resembles a small constellation. From the rear of the stage comes a large group of actors, also with lights and lanterns; it is a distant planet in another galaxy (it is also Mars). The spaceship and the

215

planet approach each other; the actors forming the spaceship de-
liver the text as their formation moves through the auditorium
and merges with the planet. The image developed by the text: The
voyage into outer space, inner space in which the unimaginable is
encountered and understood.

Action: "Fly . . . Expand Consciousness . . . Be the unalienated . . .
Go far out . . ."
 The revolution of Being, its object is the expansion of the human
potential: this could lead to flying . . .
 The performers seek a high point in the theatre's architecture.
As an actor or a member of the public prepares to leap from it, he
inhales deeply three times and then plunges into the arms of other
performers waiting below to catch him. This breathing preparation
is accompanied by a gentle, breathful rhythmic chant from those
below: Breath . . . Breath . . . Breath . . . Fly! . . . softly spoken,
the words are repeated as each person takes his position to fly.
Flash-out.
 The Action lasts as long as there are participants who wish to
perform it, or until the people catching the bodies begin to tire.
The purpose of The Flying is to lead toward a state of physical glow.

RUNG EIGHT

The Rite of I and Thou

From their positions at the end of the Revolution of Transformation
the actors begin an Om and move to the center of the area. Over-
whelmed by the death image, they begin an enactment of death; they
grow weak, breath stops, sight goes, and the world is cut off from
them. Still making the sound, they sink down, as if sinking into the
earth, and give the death signal, passing their last energy and vibrations to those around them. At this moment they have made
contact with one another, and out of this contact they are revived; in
giving each other the last of their energy, they are thereby recharged
and rise up, erect, alive, reborn. Flash-out. It is the image of death
forestalled and overcome in the contact between I and Thou.

216

The Vision of the Undoing of the Myth of Eden

The performers form a tree; it is the Tree of Knowledge. Those representing its upper branches are carried on the shoulders of those forming the trunk. The text spoken from the Tree outlines all that has been contained in the course of the play, and parts of all of its Rites and Visions are given brief, sequential flash-back re-enactments. Beginning with "I'm not allowed to take my clothes off," the text proceeds fairly rapidly to the I-Thou sequence and ends with the words: "How the Tree of Knowledge becomes the Tree of Life." The Tree is then disassembled and the actors move among the public, leaving the stage and moving toward the exits of the theatre. They carry members of the audience on their shoulders or are carried on the shoulders of the spectators.

Action: As the actors lead the public toward the exits of the theatre, they speak the following text:
The street . . .
Free the theatre . . . the theatre of the street . . . free the street.
How the Rite of I and Thou and the Vision of Paradise, of the Undoing of the Myth of Eden, can lead to the permanent revolution . . .
Theatre is in the street. . . .
The street belongs to the people. . . .
Free the theatre. . . .
Free the street. . . .
Begin.

217

The Way Back

Monday, March 10; the day before leaving San Francisco. For the first time on the tour things are being lost or misplaced, left in someone else's car, the car key is locked inside, Gianfranco leaves his wallet in Ferlinghetti's apartment and has to drive back for it at 3:00 A.M.; in packing, it is discovered that my favorite "security" sweater is missing and was probably left behind two weeks before in the Berkeley hotel . . . and time is wasted in a furious urge to spend it. Departure Anxiety, the not-so-unconscious wish to stay. It is the wish to not begin a trip that bridges a present with a future that breaks with the past.

Tuesday, March 11. Up at nine "to get an early start"— last minute good-byes, the car must be packed, some things must be claimed from a shop which is closed. It all must be carried out with determination; don't look back, you may not leave.

By 2:30 that afternoon we are on the road, eastward bound.

Eastern California could be Kansas. "Get your kicks on Route 66," a lullaby from late childhood; the bleached tones of the Arizona desert where we stop in the sun and lunch on avocados and cheese. Speeding on, a coyote gallops across the road ahead, a roadrunner darts into a clump of cactus. New Mexico: Watch A Real Indian Weaving A Real Indian Rug the billboards promise; others announce the upcoming "trading post" of Chief Yellowhorse; warm desert sun. The night is spent in a motel whose cabins are concrete wigwams. In the Office wigwam there is a notice that Eldridge Cleaver is WANTED with a reward for information leading to the arrest and conviction of the best-selling author.

Thursday, March 13. A side trip to Santa Fe where we spend the late afternoon looking at Indian objects in the shops around the old square, and the San Juan pueblo en route to Taos. . . . Taos, snug and silent in the mountain-night; the late weather report changes our minds about driving north over the mountains tomorrow. Snow storms are on the way. In the morning we head south, back to 66, according to the road map the best route in the area, and also because I'm convinced that, as such, 66 will be clear of snow when all else is buried in it. . . .

Just south of Santa Fe we hit a blinding blizzard, and it is by pure psychic radar that we locate 66 at all. 66 does happen not to have much snow—it has all turned to ice. Deep, clean, unsanded ice. The winds are very impressive, too.

The Texas Panhandle: gale winds blowing us sideways through a magna-blizzard, the ice on the windshield wipers freezing to that on the windshield; the only stretches having been sanded are those few miles through even fewer towns. It is an act of God that keeps old 66 beneath the car. Averaging forty miles-per-hour, we stop that night in a Shamrock,

220

Texas, motel. The tube tells us that 66 through the Panhandle is being closed to all traffic . . . the first of the blizzards has hit, worse expected for tomorrow, they are moving east.

This is followed by a news editorial in which a demented looking commentator rages for a quarter-of-an-hour about shoplifting and petty thievery. He's equipped with about a shopping bag-worth of charts and papers which he flails around in total outrage and indignation, as if kleptomania were a personal affront, and since he's wont to imply that much of his information has not been made available before, I begin to suspect that he has stolen it. He adjusts his eyeglasses authoritatively before cresting with the results of a private poll that show that one-out-of-every-four Americans admits to stealing regularly and that three-out-of-four admit that they would steal if they had a chance—admissions which I interpreted as indicating a lot more honesty than you'd expect to find in this country. He caps this with *government findings* . . . government findings are always more far out . . . showing that shoplifting and petty stealing offenses outnumber crimes of rape, murder, kidnapping, arson, and drug abuse by a ratio so enormous that I was gasping for breath and missed it.

Don't misunderstand: I am as shocked as the next person to hear that one-out-of-four Americans is stealing regularly. I thought the proportion was higher than that. I'm probably one of those three-out-of-four who'd steal if they had the chance, but it's crazy to watch this Irate Citizen carrying on about stealing from department stores and supermarkets when what he refers to as "the prime offenders,"

221

Americans living in ghetto poverty, would find honesty like this just another luxury; to hear him forcing a comparison between shoplifting or petty stealing and the murderous crimes when his statistics for the latter have failed to include those committed in Vietnam. He concludes by urging us to report these pilferous crimes whenever we see them being committed. He says this is one good solution, which shows a clear misinterpretation of information. Conclusion Based On The Given Data: Stealing is good for the economy; it's nonviolent and it keeps merchandise in circulation.

Saturday, March 15, 9:30 A.M. Today's task is to out-drive the weather. By the time we reach the Texas-Oklahoma border the snow has stopped, or hasn't started yet, if weather predictions hold, but it rains heavily all the way to Okla-homa City, tapering off by Tulsa. Dry and overcast; a for-tuitous lack of weather. Dinner that night in a St. Louis suburb where a road sign says Pizzeria and Italian Restau-rant. Another instance of mid-American anomaly, this is obviously THE place to be seen on Saturday night in St. Louis. A dietic slice of life, the Midwestern avant-society: well-preserved matrons in a rainbow of crotch-length stretch boots and mini-skirts that graze the kneecap; middle-aged businessmen in dinner jackets, ascots, turtlenecks and discreetly ruffled shirts, and argyle socks; the female de-vouring her prey in a raucously babbling maw. Dressed for the road and not bothering to change, the zap of it all having stunned the maître d' into letting us in, we are seated at a candlelit table in the midst of the din, which undulates into dead silence when every eye has plugged into us. The interest in exoticism isn't mutual, and sensing this, resenting it, they

222

try to recapture the attention misspent on us. Their loud remarks aren't clever, their intended insults unimaginative, attempts at conviviality clumsy and uncalled for. The waiter is so aggressively nice; will we really need all of these little butter pats and napkins and utensils? Faceless Strangers Forever, please try to understand: we are happy in our isolation from you and do not want your crippled egos any more than we want A.1. Sauce for our pizza; we are tired and wish to be ignored. The exposure of yet more dreary souls . . . you are the trees that we happen to hear when you fall in the empty forest.

The decision is reached when the coffee is brought: to dex and drive through the night. . . .

Illinois . . . Indiana: I sleep through it, awakening at 4:00 A.M. in time to be WELCOME TO OHIO, and reset my watch to coincide with the loss of another hour in the amenity . . . Cincinnati, 6:00 A.M.; a rosy-fingered dawn. And Dawn fingered her back . . . breakfast in an unrecorded Ohio town which, for all we know (or care), may have been the cradle of civilization . . . a sliver of West Virginia and a touch of spring in the sunny Sunday mid-morning. . . . For the third time in four months, the Pennsylvania Turnpike and the rolling Pennsylvania hills; without the snow of the previous trips they are gentle, tame. The temptation to make comparisons: it is like New Mexico with trees instead of cacti, it is like Ohio only with hills. But it's not. The familiarity of the East Coast terrain is comforting, if unexciting. Before leaving the turnpike at Harrisburg, we're stopped by a traffic cop who tells us politely that we shouldn't be doing more than seventy in a VW. We're glad to get out of the car

223

and stretch our legs. Harrisburg to New Jersey, route signs Watch For Left Turns and Cross Traffic, soothing us by the absence of the SLIDES and FLASH FLOODS of the West, signalling that the eastern geography is under control: we must just watch out for each other.

Late afternoon sun slants across New Jersey, an unfamiliar part that looks like Ohio with hills, or Vermont with lower ones. Before belaboring comparisons, it changes . . . a Sunday evening traffic jam and Total Jersey. Newark and a short stretch of turnpike to the Lincoln Tunnel . . . cars careening in and out of lanes, herds of trucks and buses scorch past at ninety miles an hour. They will kill anyone who tries to stop them . . . signal lights winking furiously in the fading dusklight, flirting with time to trifle with space, seduced by both. In tandem. Less than a dozen miles from New York space runs out and it takes two hours to get to the Lincoln Tunnel and into the city. We arrive home around 8:00, direct from Shamrock, Texas, Sunday evening, March 16.

The company returned to the East Coast for its last performances in America, two nights at Boston's Ark Theatre, and an overly publicized disruption of the Theatre of Ideas (after which the Living Theatre was branded "fascist," as if there were not enough to worry about already), prior to beginning a nine-day return engagement at the Brooklyn Academy of Music. The fact that from the proceeds of these final two weeks it was able to pay off the balance owned on the tour's tax bill and what was owed for the return fares to Europe, plus all of the salaries in arrears to the actors, would indicate that had things been properly managed from the outset, the terrible financial difficulties could have been avoided. The system they so valiantly struggled against had made a stronger point than it should have been permitted.

But the accumulated stress of the past months, the discouragements and the disasters of California, the last-minute interviews and meetings in New York, the final preparations for departure—they all took their toll on Julian. On closing night as the set was being struck for the last time, Julian—having distributed the boat and plane tickets and paid the salaries, having gone on for the final standing-room-only performance of *Frankenstein,* having once again taken care of the reality bag, collapsed in the dressing room. Driven back to his mother's home in New York City, he remained there under medical care until the Monday morning departure.

Monday, March 31. A morning similar to six months ago when the sky was clear and bright and the air held a promise of a new season, and the Living arrived with a flamboyant Presence that had flowed out and created a sense of anticipation for what the new season would bring. In the time elapsed expectation has turned to uncertainty, and on board the *Europa* today the mood is subdued, there is less bustling confusion than there was then, and fewer people have come to say good-bye or to record the departure for mass posterity.

Relief, release, quiet joy, and a certain sadness; it is over at last and much has been lost. And something gained, but it's too soon to know exactly what, exactly how each in his own private being will absorb the experience. Loss is more strongly sensed because it is closer and must be assimilated fully before the gain can be understood. Somehow they will survive . . . collective survival may in itself be the singular gain . . . one senses that, too, as the other passengers eye them curiously with bewilderment and a touch of suspicion in their gaze. Through the cautious attention of these strangers, German-speaking and Teutonically crisp in appearance, the Presence is gradually recovered, reflecting and asserting itself wearily amidst the commotion of the others on board. The Presence, the persona of the Living, so flamboyantly cohesive six months ago, is tired now, a bit shabby and less "together" in spirit, but as if specializing in arrivals and departures, it is once again invented and transmitted through the reaction of strangers to its individual components. It is this externally imposed insularity that could perpetuate their collective survival.

As all departures are attractive for the idea of movement and enviable for the implied mobility of those in-transit, this morning is not without its out-of-transit frustrations. But excitement is tempered by a sense of sadness that lies beneath the restrained jubilation of the Living. With all its triumphs and defeats, the American visit is finally over and they are happy to be leaving. Destination: France for a six-week tour, to be followed by a month of performances in London; then the filming of *Paradise Now* might begin, or the filming of *Frankenstein* might begin, it all depends on if and when and which, if either, of the negotiations are completed. If the films are postponed, an offer to perform again in Yugoslavia might be accepted. After London, nothing is definite,

226

but it doesn't matter, it is too far ahead. The present, this sea-borne "between," must be held as long as possible, for the future is uncertain and so much must be restored before it can be grasped.

The *Europa* has sailed.

Julian's Tape: The Last Word

The following is from a two-part telecast on the Living Theatre by San Francisco's educational channel KQED-TV. Having videotaped a lecture-demonstration at Mills College and parts from *Mysteries* in the KQED studios the previous day, this interview with Julian Beck took place on March 9 in Golden Gate Park. The interviewer is program producer Robert Hagopian.

Interviewer: Julian, you left this country when the IRS closed you down in New York. You've come back and you're still facing tax troubles. Why *did* you come back?

Julian: The company travels wherever it's invited. It's a little bit like a ship without an anchor. We groove very much on traveling around, it's our pleasure. We had been in Europe for four and a half years, and eventually this invitation came to come back for a six-month tour of the States, and so we did. It seemed perfectly natural.

Interviewer: Have you found many changes in the United States that you see now and the one you left four and a half years ago?

Julian: What seems to me the most significant thing is

the development of an actively revolutionary youth, of an anarchist foundation dissatisfied not only with the current structure of society, but with some ideas which are clearly forming themselves toward a real social restructure. This seems to me the most significant change. There are other groups which are aligned, and perhaps in a certain sense we're all together. Perhaps some of them are a little less definite in their direction, in their vectors, and are a little screwed up on the crucial subject of violence, but that seems to me natural. The violence rises out of despair and out of ten thousand years of civilization which has told us that violence is the means to solving problems. The real revolution, I think, is a totally counter-violent revolution.

Interviewer: You use the word "anarchist" and in one of your productions there is much talk of "anarchy." The dictionary says that anarchy is one, the absence of government; and two, a kind of political disorder. How do you view "anarchy"?

Julian: Classically, the word comes from the Greek and it means simply "without an archon," without a head that is controlling things. What we're looking forward to is a system in which the people take care of themselves without designating abstract forms to control them—small communities in which we can get to communicate with each other and tell each other what our needs are. Obviously with the help of cybernetic automation to process these needs, and then to produce what's necessary—food, clothing, heat— and to distribute them free. That should take about ten percent of the labor time that we now expend in our commercial endeavors, and then [we can] get on to other things.

Interviewer: Your theatre really criticizes the foundations of our society. Robert Brustein at the end of his book *Theatre of Revolt* says that one thing he found that people ask when you kick at the foundations of society is: What does the artist have to offer in place of those foundations? When you and your company talk to audiences do you find that they ask you that kind of question? In other words, what would you put in place of the foundation?

Julian: We are asked that question in a very curious fashion, as if there were no answer. This is because the programming, the un-free education is such that it teaches nothing except how-to-fit-into-the-present-structure, as if that were the only solution. I think this is one of the reasons why students today are protesting the whole educational system—because it is a *system,* and it educates you to take your place in a system. It is also a system that educates a privileged few. It is not free education, it is not for the greater part of the people. There are millions who are simply disinherited, who are culturally, educationally underprivileged. A form of violence is done to them, while the others who have sufficient money or background in order to get into a school are then processed. As in the army, they are taught how to run that system so that it keeps controlling the whole human spirit.

Interviewer: Eric Bentley has said that he thinks that Madison Avenue is now the seat of education for the entire world. Do you think this is true?

Julian: I think that Madison Avenue serves very much

as the medium of expression for capitalism and the state. That is, it gives out all the propaganda. In general, this propaganda tells people they are very stupid, because the Madison Avenue formulae and the devices they use are all stupid-making devices. . . . They advertise products in a stupid manner, they ferret their way into certain areas of the brain, and in a sense, they capitalize on the stupidity of people, incrementing and increasing it. All of the media do this . . . television, radio, the newspapers, the magazines, films . . . so that part of [our] work is to assault the culture, to change the culture, and to change the means of communication.

Here is a holy thing, communication between people, and it is being used to make people *greedier*. The whole capitalistic system makes people greedier and gets them hung up on a lower consciousness, desiring more and more materials and thinking that's the answer to life. Furthermore, it keeps filtering out in various insidious ways, a propaganda to maintain loyalty to the status quo. Now the status quo we know is a failure. We know that capitalism is a failure, we know that the modern state is a failure . . . and we know this because every four seconds one person dies of starvation, because the exploitation and the wars persist, the unhappiness persists, yet we constantly think that through ameliorative processes and reformist measures we can have a better democracy; *if only we had a better President everything would be cool!* But for ten thousand years we have been waiting for a better President, a better King. There are no better kings. There are only the people and the people can do for themselves. The people have the power, but the kings,

the presidents, the senates and the senators are always tell-
ing them that they *don't* have the power, that they can't ad-
ministrate for themselves, that they can't do it, and *this* is
what we have to change.

Interviewer: Is there a difference in the spirit of audiences
in this country and that of audiences in Europe?

Julian: In a real sense, no. This question is always asked
as we travel around . . . there are the obvious geographic
differences; an audience in southern Italy or in Sicily is going
to be very lively and talkative, because that's their way. An
audience of Swedes is just going to sit there and watch.
They'll be totally expressionless but they'll dig it, because
that's the form that, in a sense, the society takes.

The significant thing, I think, is that everywhere in all
of the large cities . . . and it is essentially in the large cities
where IT is happening . . . internationally the big cities are
the center of revolutionary response and action.

Interviewer: I'd like to ask you about the art of your
theatre. Degas said: "Art is impossible without virtuosity."
How do you build virtuosity into your company? Your
people do tremendous things in performance. Is there a
training program? How do you do this?

Julian: No, not really. The general principle is simply to
create an atmosphere in which the individual is free to create,
in which he's not dictated to, but in which he is able to draw
upon his own resources, his own imagination, in which he
is simply *free* to get those creative juices going. It seems
then to spill out in plethora. The problem is . . . how would
you say? . . . *to select* from this kind of ample cornucopia. I
think the real work of the director in the modern theatre is

233

to eliminate himself, and if he can't do that, then at least to establish inside the acting company a situation in which the actor is total artist, is able to take more and more control of the total work, rather than being a puppet within some kind of diagram.

Interviewer: When you're invited to perform is the invitation most often for the company or for a particular play?

Julian: Generally for the company.

Interviewer: About your repertory, do you and Judith Malina do the writing?

Julian: No, not really . . . the plays have been created collectively. That is, we sit around with the company during very long extended rehearsal periods, and we talk and we talk and we talk until the ideas evolve.

Interviewer: *Antigone* has been criticized for the way your company handled the speech of classical theatre. In much modern theatre the direction is away from the importance of speech and of a script. Can this direction be justified?

Julian: Yes. There are two things about it. One is that the whole form of theatrical speech is something that we want to get rid of. It's a kind of artificiality, a kind of *regality*. That is, the way an actor generally speaks is very closely related to the *ancien régime* idea of the way the king speaks. For example, John Gielgud speaks like The King . . . he holds up for the spectator constantly this model of the perfect molding of the English language as spoken by "King." What we need now is to get away from the formal husking of the voice in the throat. We have to get to a more natural kind of speech, a more imaginative kind of speech, a more imaginative use of the vocal chords, of the whole voice box which, in general, is just too much a means of conveying cerebral symbols: the words come out.

The other thing is that we rely on the words for communication rather than on the tone or on the expression rising out of the body and the mind. The voice box is [regarded as] a thing that's separate from the body itself, as the brain has become a thing that's separate from the body itself. Yet the brain is a biological entity, it's existing, living matter, and it's been very badly programmed. The brain is a great computer beyond computers, and yet it's fed totally with false information.

We really don't feel; we're a feelingless people. We don't see; we're aware of that. Our perception is limited. Our hearing is limited; we don't hear. For hundreds of years we were unable to hear the cry of the black man, because we're *deaf,* and it's just beginning to reach us because he's screaming loud enough. As a consequence . . . because we can't feel, because we don't see, because we don't hear . . . we're giving all the wrong information to the brain so that the words, which are the result of the rational process coming out, are all inexact, are all false information. We, the Living Theatre, are trying to reach toward some kind of communication of feeling and idea that push toward some other area that is beneath words or beyond words, or *in addition to words.* The object is not to destroy language. . . . I think that man's greatest creation is speech, but the object is to deepen it and to amplify it and to make the communication real rather than a series of lies.

Interviewer: You've also been criticized for the way you

235

treat an audience, and yet your theatre audiences are invited to participate, they've even been invited on the stage. How do you feel about this criticism?

Julian: Well, I find it's a very common thing among our critics. It goes something like this: The Living Theatre is too violent, they're always yelling at the audience, always screaming at the audience, kicking, smashing, and so forth. This kind of complaint is true of all forms of the establishment. That is, the establishment, the governments, which are the prime examples of the uses of violence . . . your government wages its wars; your capitalism exploits its people; your United Fruit and your coffee companies exploit the peasants who spend their lives picking the bananas and picking the coffee beans and sleep in nothing but mud huts before dying at the age of forty from various diseases. But these establishment people are the first to say violence, violence.

The students begin to get excited, they get angry, and they say No, no, no; we will not be trained to take part in such a system. Mr. Nixon says violence; we must have law and order. . . . *His* law and *his* order, which are the most unlawful and most un-orderly imaginable. . . . There is no law and order in Vietnam, absolutely none. There is no law and order in the life on the black ghetto; these people live in total disorder, mocked by law and justice.

The critic, too . . . as soon as an actor begins to scream at him about the anguish and the pain that he feels a relationship to, that he knows in the world, the critic—who wants the calm, intellectual, bourgeois theatre that puts forth an intellectual problem which one can go home and

236

think and do nothing about, never take action on—he is the one who immediately says violence, that's bad, very bad. It's part of the strategy of the revolution to get people to declare themselves, to show where they are. Even if they do this through lies . . . because that is their way . . . or inexactitudes, because they cannot see. The rest of us are able to see what's really going on.

Interviewer: You're going back to France now. Are your plays the same there? Is the subject matter the same wherever you play?

Julian: Yes. We're doing the same plays here that we developed in Europe, and we do them the same way there, except that over there we work much more in the languages of the countries.

Interviewer: Are there any plans to come back for another tour?

Julian: Right now, if we want it, we have a number of years of work abroad, and we'll just see what happens. As I say, we've gotten a little bit past, at least for ourselves, the chauvinistic idea that you have to be in your own country all the time, that anybody who leaves his country is somehow or other doing the wrong thing. Wherever we go, that's our country. One has to get rid of the borders.

Interviewer: Is there any place in this country where you felt that you really had an unusual, a more genuine response than you're used to?

Julian: No. I like the phrase of Bertolt Brecht's: "One place is as bad as another."

The Living Theatre Itinerary:
September 1968–March 1969

9 September . . . Arrived in New York aboard the Italian liner *Aurelia*

September

16	Yale School of Drama	MYSTERIES AND
	New Haven, Connecticut	SMALLER PIECES
17	"	"
18	"	"
19	"	ANTIGONE
20	"	"
21	"	"
23	"	FRANKENSTEIN
24	"	"
25	"	"
26	"	PARADISE NOW (BUST)
27	"	"
28	"	"

October

2	Brooklyn Academy of Music,	
	Brooklyn, New York	FRANKENSTEIN
3		"
4	"	"
5	"	"
6	"	"
7	"	"

239

9	*"*	MYSTERIES
10	*"*	ANTIGONE
11	*"*	*"*
12	*"*	MYSTERIES (MAT.) / ANTIGONE
13	*"*	ANTIGONE *"* / MYSTERIES
14	*"*	PARADISE
16	*"*	*"*
17	*"*	MYSTERIES
18	*"*	PARADISE
19	*"*	ANTIGONE (MAT.) / PARADISE
20	*"*	MYSTERIES *"* / *"*
21	*"*	PARADISE

27 Becks interviewed by *Newsweek's* Jack Kroll, and company performs the "Brig Dollar" and "The Plague" from *Mysteries* for CBS-TV videotaping of *Camera 3* program; two-part show was telecast January 12 and 19 (1969).

28	State Univ. at Stony Brook; Stony Brook, Long Island	MYSTERIES
29	*"*	PARADISE
31	Kresge Auditorium, M.I.T., Cambridge, Massachusetts	FRANKENSTEIN

November

1	*"*	*"*
3	*"*	MYSTERIES (MAT.) /
5	*"*	*"*
6	Brown University, Providence, Rhode Island	PARADISE
7–8	Performances scheduled for these dates at the Kresge Auditorium, *Antigone* & *Paradise* respectively, canceled by M.I.T. administration.	

12	Goddard College,	
	Plainview, Vermont	MYSTERIES
14	Carnegie-Mellon University,	
	Pittsburgh, Pa.	MYSTERIES
15	"	PARADISE
18	Rutgers Univ., New Jersey	lecture-demonstration by company
20	Castleton State Teachers	
	College, Castleton, Vermont	PARADISE
21	Bennington College,	"
	Bennington, Vermont	
22	Smith College;	lecture-demonstration
	North Hampton, Mass.	by company
24	YM-YWHA,	
	Philadelphia, Pa.	ANTIGONE
25	"	FRANKENSTEIN
26	"	PARADISE (BUST)
30	Princeton University,	
	Princeton, New Jersey	MYSTERIES

December

1	Great Neck Community Center,	
	Great Neck, Long Island	ANTIGONE
2	University of Scranton,	
	Scranton, Pa.	MYSTERIES
4	Denison University,	
	Granville, Ohio	"
6	Playhouse-in-the-Park,	
	Cincinnati, Ohio	FRANKENSTEIN
7	"	MYSTERIES (MAT.)/ ANTIGONE
10	University of Michigan,	
	Ann Arbor, Mich.	MYSTERIES
11	"	PARADISE
12	Detroit Institute of Art,	
	Detroit, Mich.	MYSTERIES
13	"	ANTIGONE
14	"	FRANKENSTEIN

241

16	Willard Straight Hall, Cornell University, Ithaca, New York	MYSTERIES
17	University of Rochester, Rochester, New York	PARADISE
18	Cornell University	"
21	John Hancock Hall (Roxbury), Boston	ANTIGONE
22	"	PARADISE
24	Poe Forum, Bronx, New York	FRANKENSTEIN
25	"	"
26	"	"
27	"	MYSTERIES
28	"	ANTIGONE
29	"	PARADISE
31	"	MYSTERIES

January

1	"	PARADISE
2	Hunter College, New York	ANTIGONE
3	"	MYSTERIES
4	"	PARADISE
7	University of Chicago	MYSTERIES
8	"	ANTIGONE
9	"	FRANKENSTEIN
10	"	"
11	"	MYSTERIES
12	"	PARADISE
15	Unitarian Church, Madison, Wisconsin	ANTIGONE
16	"	PARADISE
16	Lawrence University, Appleton, Wisconsin	MYSTERIES
17	"	FRANKENSTEIN
22	State University of Iowa, Iowa City, Iowa	MYSTERIES (MAT.)/ ANTIGONE
24	Civic Center, Chicago, Illinois	PARADISE

28	Soldiers & Sailors Memorial Hall, Kansas City, Kansas	MYSTERIES
29	*"*	ANTIGONE
30	*"*	PARADISE

February

2	Fort Hays State College, Fort Hays, Kansas	MYSTERIES
4	Colo. State Univ., Fort Collins, Colorado	ANTIGONE
5	University of Colorado, Boulder, Colorado	FRANKENSTEIN
6	*"*	PARADISE
11	Reed College; Portland, Oregon	MYSTERIES
12	*"*	*"*
13	*"*	PARADISE
14	*"*	ANTIGONE
16	Ashland University, Ashland, Oregon	*"*
18	Berkeley Community Theatre, Berkeley, California	MYSTERIES
19	*"*	FRANKENSTEIN
20	*"*	PARADISE (!??!!)
24	University of Southern California, Los Angeles, California	MYSTERIES
25	*"*	FRANKENSTEIN
26	*"*	*"*
27	*"*	ANTIGONE
28	*"*	PARADISE

March

1–2 *Mysteries* and *Paradise*, respectively, scheduled for these dates canceled by dean of USC.

243

4	Straight Theatre, San Francisco	free performance. . . . *Space to the Spaced*
5	Nourse Auditorium, San Francisco	ANTIGONE
6	"	FRANKENSTEIN
7	"	PARADISE
8	"	"

Lecture-demonstration at Mills College in morning; in afternoon, videotaping of the "Brig Dollar," "The Chord" and "The Plague," all from *Mysteries,* by San Francisco's educational TV channel KGED

11	eastward bound	
19	Ark Theatre, Boston	MYSTERIES
20	"	ANTIGONE
21	Guest appearances at Theatre of Ideas, New York	
22	Brooklyn Academy of Music	PARADISE
23	"	"
24	"	"
25	"	FRANKENSTEIN
26	"	PARADISE
27	Brooklyn College; matinee at BAM	MYSTERIES ANTIGONE
28	"	FRANKENSTEIN
29	"	"
31	Company sails for France aboard the German liner *Europa.*	

On May 24, 1969, the Living Theatre was given three Off-Broadway awards, or "Obies," including the $500 Plumsock Award for *Frankenstein.* The other two awards went to Julian Beck for his brilliant portrayal of Creon in *Antigone* and to Judith Malina for her performance in the title role of the same.

244

Bibliography

Artaud, Antonin. *Le Théâtre et Son Double*. Paris: Gallimard, 1938.

Avalon, Arthur (Sir John Woodroffe). *Le Puissance du Serpent*. Lyon: Paul Derain, 1959.

Biner, Pierre. *Le Living Théâtre*. Lausanne: La Cité, 1968.

Brown, Kenneth H. *The Brig*. With an Introduction by Julian Beck. New York: Hill and Wang, 1965.

Laing, R. D. *The Politics of Experience & The Bird of Paradise*. London: Penguin Books, 1967.

Living Theatre Poems. New York: Boss Books, 1969.

Marcuse, Herbert. *Eros and Civilization*. Boston: Beacon Press, 1966.

City Lights Journal, Number Three. City Lights Books, San Francisco.

Index

247

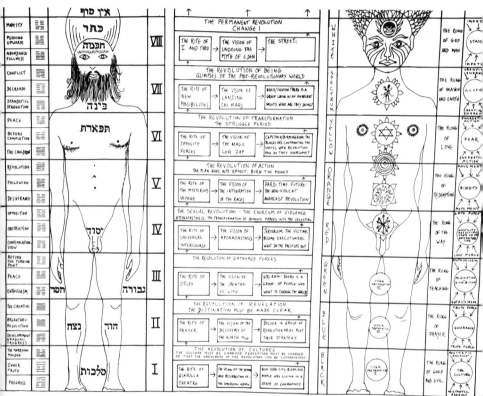

THIS CHART IS THE MAP

THE LIVING THEATRE

THE ESSENTIAL TRIP IS THE VOYAGE FROM THE MANY TO THE ONE

PARADISE NOW

THE PLOT IS THE REVOLUTION

COLLECTIVE CREATION